A Dog Named Leaf

ALSO BY ALLEN AND LINDA ANDERSON

Angel Dogs: Divine Messengers of Love

Dogs and the Women Who Love Them: Extraordinary True Stories of Loyalty, Healing & Inspiration

Rescued: Saving Animals from Disaster

Angel Dogs with a Mission: Divine Messengers in Service to All Life

Saying Goodbye to Your Angel Animals: Finding Comfort After Losing Your Pet

Animals and the Kids Who Love Them: Extraordinary True Stories of Hope, Healing, and Compassion

Angel Horses: Divine Messengers of Hope

Angel Cats: Divine Messengers of Comfort

Horses with a Mission: Extraordinary True Stories of Equine Service

Angel Animals: Divine Messengers of Miracles

Angel Animals Book of Inspiration: Divine Messengers of Wisdom and Compassion

Rainbows & Bridges: An Animal Companion Memorial Kit

A Dog Named Leaf

The Hero from Heaven Who Saved My Life

Allen Anderson with Linda Anderson

LYONS PRESS
Guilford, Connecticut
An imprint of Globe Pequot Press

Some names and details concerning private individuals and the chronology of certain events have been changed. A Dog Named Leaf: The Hero from Heaven Who Saved My Life *is based on the authors' memories and interpretations of events.*

To buy books in quantity for corporate use or incentives, call **(800) 962–0973** or e-mail **premiums@GlobePequot.com.**

Lyons Press is an imprint of Globe Pequot Press.

Interior photos by Allen Anderson except pages 48 and 180, Patrycia Miller, owner of Pampered Pooch Playground and Bubbly Paws, www.pamperedpoochplayground.com; front cover and page 201, Peter Crouser, www.petercrouser.com; and page 213 Kristy Walker, www.kristywalker.com

Design: Sheryl P. Kober
Project editor: Julie Marsh
Layout: Sue Murray

Library of Congress Cataloging-in-Publication Data is available on file.

ISBN 978-0-7627-8165-2

Printed in the United States of America

10 9 8 7 6 5 4 3 2 1

Contents

Preface

"Nothing is as important as going home at the end of your watch. Nothing."

My mentor, Bruce Mathis, an experienced police officer, once said these wise words to me, a rookie cop, during one of our patrols together.

Unlike some veterans I'd spent time with, Bruce had not grown cynical and jaded after seeing firsthand the worst in human nature. Instead, he was respectful and gracious with everyone. He often flashed a crooked grin that revealed his quirky sense of humor and defused tension in stressful situations. I was nervous about doing a good job, but being around Bruce put me at ease.

One afternoon while Bruce and I patrolled his regular beat, a middle-class residential area, the horn of our police car started beeping on its own. A middle-aged couple looked up from weeding flowers in their front yard. They must have thought we honked the police car horn at them, so they waved at us. Bruce and I smiled and waved back. Two blocks down the road, our horn beeped again. Several people standing at a bus stop looked at us. One gave a hesitant wave.

As the horn continued its beeping, we passed seniors taking leisurely walks. They waved and smiled at us. We waved and smiled back at them. "It's an electrical short," Bruce said, laughing. "Looks like we're Officer Friendly today." For the remaining hour of our shift, Bruce's horn beeped every five to ten minutes. We continued to patrol the neighborhood like homecoming queens waving from a parade float.

During my week riding in his patrol car, I came to think of Bruce as a friend. He seemed to have taken a liking to me too. Before I took my first solo assignment in a busy, more crime-filled zone than his, Bruce said, "I live for my wife and child. They are everything to me." He added, "Nothing is as important as going home at the end of your watch. Nothing."

Although my sparse bachelor's apartment wasn't much to go home to, I thought I understood what he meant.

Three years later, while moonlighting as a security guard at Lenox Square, a mega-mall in Atlanta, a burglar shot Bruce. He'd surprised the thief in a large, isolated storage room. From what I heard later, by the time someone found him, it was too late. Bruce was only in his midthirties. Grief-stricken and enraged after the news about his death circulated through the police station, I sat in my patrol car and asked, "Why?"

During the funeral I glanced over at Bruce's wife, a young woman in her twenties. She looked broken. Her eyes were reddened by the flow of tears. Her child, now fatherless, stood motionless. Bruce had provided the content of her life. Now she looked as empty as a book with blank pages.

By the time of Bruce's death, I had recently married my amazing, talented, and beautiful wife Linda. I had adopted Susan and Mun, the two children she had adopted from Korea. I loved my new family with all my heart. Would they one day stand like Bruce's wife and young child, facing life without me? Then I remembered Bruce's rule. I would do everything in my power to stay safe.

Soon after Bruce died I answered a routine call for suspicious drug activity by several young males. I pulled up in my patrol car without my sirens blaring or blue lights flashing. It was dusk, and shafts of sunlight filtered through the clouds. When I exited the car, three young men immediately scattered in different directions.

I don't know what compelled me, but I took off on foot after one of them. Normally I would have gotten more information from the person who had called the police. The men probably lived in this housing project, and someone would know them. Instead, I gave chase like a dog running after a thrown tennis ball. I even thought, *This is not who I am. Be careful.* Still, I ran faster.

The man I was chasing suddenly flashed around the corner of the apartment building, and I lost sight of him. It was getting darker. It occurred to me that I might slam into a wire clothesline or trip over scattered debris. I even heard what sounded like Bruce's voice shouting "Stop!" But that didn't stop me. I had to catch this guy.

Around the corner, about twenty-five feet away, the man crouched behind the apartment building. He pointed his gun directly at my head. I was out in the open. No cover. I clumsily grabbed my gun out of my holster, raised my firearm, and aimed at him. And waited. The young man slowly lowered the weapon to his side. But he kept it firmly locked in his hand.

A second police unit pulled into the housing project right then, and Officer Jackson, a husky man in his late twenties, jumped out of the car. He had a reputation for overreacting and occasionally using excessive force at any hint of resistance, so I was worried about what he might do. Jackson ran toward me, and we both aimed our guns at the young man. I yelled, "Drop it!"

In the longest two seconds of my life, I waited. At last, the man placed his gun down on the dry, hard dirt. Jackson and I cuffed him. While we walked him to the police unit, I read the man his rights. Jackson shoved the subject into the back of the patrol car. He looked at me and said, "This could have been a good shooting." He was talking about shooting an armed man who had refused to drop his weapon. If our lives had been in jeopardy at any time during the incident, use of deadly force would have been justified.

"You take it," I told Jackson, giving credit for the arrest to him. I felt embarrassed. How stupid of me to chase the guy. I walked to my car, shaking my head. "Why didn't he shoot?"

Some would say I was lucky. Some would say I was protected. Others might say I was just a stupid young cop. I think it might be a combination of all three. I felt gratitude for the God-given protection that made it possible for me to go home one more night to my wife and children.

Over my eight years as a police officer, I was spared many times from being injured or killed. Linda began calling me "Miracle Man." I silently repeated Bruce's rule at the beginning of each shift. In my mind's eye I saw his big easy smile, as he reminded me to never forget it.

Years later there would be another kind of weapon aimed at my head with its trigger cocked. My new situation would be as life threatening as any I'd faced while doing police work. I would be in a different city, with my children grown. My wife and I would have embarked on a new path of writing, not mystery novels but animal books. Into that mix there would come a dog who was like none I'd ever known. This book tells the extraordinary true story of that rescued dog who stood between the threat of death and me—and how we made a pact to help each other survive.

PART ONE

The Journey of Two Souls Begins

On the path that leads to Nowhere
I have sometimes found my soul.

—CORINNE ROOSEVELT ROBINSON,
"THE PATH THAT LEADS TO NOWHERE"

Chapter One

Life as I Knew It

The day started like any other day. I sat at my desk and gazed at a cloudless, azure sky from my fourth-floor office window. A couple dozen seabirds swooped in unison over the flat plain of the Minnesota landscape dotted with tall city buildings and oak trees. I started to prepare for a client conference call scheduled for later that morning. I moved a small, framed photo of our dog Leaf's face to the right corner of my desk to make room for my notes. The image of the jet-black cocker spaniel Linda and I had adopted from an animal shelter seven months prior brought a smile to my face.

The day before, Leaf and I had visited the dog park near our home. I loved seeing the joy shine in his eager eyes and his legs tremble with excitement each time I held his favorite ball in the air. When I threw it the heavens opened up for him. Over and over, he ran after the ball, and his long, floppy ears flapped in the wind. It delighted me when he rushed back to where I waited for him. He'd drop the ball at my feet, then, with his pink tongue hanging comically out of his mouth, he'd wait for the next round of play.

I had grown to appreciate every inch of Leaf's jellyroll body. The eight-inch legs that sunk into snowdrifts. The paw he'd raise to pat my knee whenever he wanted attention. The curve of his snout, which tipped upward. The wide, black, moist, and ever-sniffing nose that gave his profile a regal bearing. The pungent odor of his perspiration. The stubby tail

that whipped in circles when he greeted my return home. The penetrating coal eyes that sparkled with personality when he'd peek at me out of the corners of his eyes or intensely examine my face for clues to my mood. All these aspects of my complex dog were becoming more welcome with each passing day.

His trust in me was not complete, though. Far from it. Even this morning he still hadn't wanted a hug or even a pat before I left for work. The cautious and guarded way that he demanded affection only on his terms made Leaf more catlike than usual for a dog. His body stiffened if I patted his head. He flinched when I tried to approach him directly or unexpectedly.

Despite his initial distrust and fear, Leaf was taking baby steps into becoming a more reliable and fun canine companion. At times he'd plop down at my feet and take in the scenery at outdoor cafes. While driving in the car at night, sometimes I would call out, "Rabbit." Then I'd point out the white-tailed bunnies I saw while Leaf's legs quivered against my shoulder.

I had left him relaxing on the couch that morning, carefully licking his furry right front paw. After the right was completely licked, he started working on the left one. I looked at him and said, "I'll be back." Whether he actually understood or not, he listened intently to my promise. I sensed that to a rescued dog, the intent behind my words meant a lot.

That morning, though, I wasn't just thinking about Leaf and how he was adjusting to life with us. I was also thinking about the puzzling bouts of dizziness I'd been having for the past few weeks. A couple of times the spells were so severe that I'd had to hold onto the wall as my body involuntarily slid down to the floor. Sensations of vertigo, claustrophobia, and spinning were happening more and more frequently. I tried to brush them off as symptoms of an inner ear infection that would heal in time. But combined with a series of disturbing dreams I'd had lately about catastrophe striking, all of this made me apprehensive about my health.

When I told Linda about my concerns, she fixed on me with her blue eyes. In an unwavering voice, she insisted that I see our family doctor right away. I thought she might be overreacting, but I've learned during the course of our marriage that if Linda is determined that something will happen, it will happen. I knew Linda would keep asking about my dizziness until I could say, "The doctor says it's nothing." And so I made an appointment to see Dr. Scott.

An older, no-nonsense fellow nearing retirement, Dr. Scott listened to my symptoms and did a thorough medical checkup. He made no comment and did not flash one of his rare smiles. "I want you to see a specialist to eliminate other reasons for your symptoms," he said. Without further explanation, he referred me to a neurologist.

The next week I went to see the neurologist, Dr. Lucas, a man in his midfifties, who sported a bushy black-and-gray mustache. He ordered an MRI-CAT scan.

That medical test was an experience I do not want to repeat—ever. My head and much of my body entered a metal tube with no more than inches of space around me. Strapped in and sweating, I felt claustrophobic. The only thing that eased my nerves was to visualize walking along an oceanfront beach with Leaf. While the loud MRI throbbed, I imagined him running in the surf, chasing birds, with no intention of catching them, and always looking back over his shoulder to make sure he didn't stray too far from me.

As I left the hospital, I told myself that the test had only been necessary to eliminate possibilities. I was probably just having too much stress at work. The strange symptoms were a fluke. Before the MRI-CAT scan results were in, my dizziness ended as mysteriously as it had begun.

Still watching the swirl of birds in the sky and preparing for my conference call, I heard the receptionist's phone buzz outside my door. She sent the call straight through to me, and I picked up.

"I'm sorry, I didn't get your name. Who is this?" I asked. I assumed it was one of my clients.

"Dr. Lucas," the voice on the phone answered. "I'm calling about your test results."

Ah, it's the neurologist making a courtesy call, I thought.

"Allen, we found something on your CAT scan."

I quickly reached over from my desk chair to close the door. I grabbed the nearest pen, which happened to have red ink, and printed the name "Dr. Lucas" across my yellow notepad.

Dr. Lucas remained silent for a moment, letting his words sink in. "It appears from the CAT scan that you have an unruptured brain aneurysm."

"Where?" I asked.

"In your *brain*," he said, emphasizing the last word.

If it hadn't been such a serious subject, I might have laughed.

Dr. Lucas continued somberly, "The aneurysm is located on the interior carotid artery. If you place your finger between your eyes, at the base of your forehead, it's about one inch deep."

I held the phone receiver with one hand and touched my forehead with the forefinger of my other hand. I quickly moved my finger away, as if I'd placed it on some odd spot where it didn't belong.

Dr. Lucas added that I was one of the fortunate few. My aneurysm had been discovered before it ruptured.

I grasped on to the word "ruptured," rolling it around in my mind. The doctor began talking about the aneurysm's size, the need for more detailed tests, the percentages of fatalities (fatalities!?), strokes, and severe disabilities from ruptured aneurysms.

Dr. Lucas said that my episodes of dizziness were not a symptom of the aneurysm. He had no explanation for why the vertigo had occurred or what made it stop. But he was glad that it had prompted me to make an appointment.

My voice broke a little when I said, "Thanks for letting me know."

"No need to panic. But this is worthy of concern," Dr. Lucas replied.

In an instant I latched on to "worthy of concern" as my first ray of hope. Lots of things are worthy of concern. Maybe a brain aneurysm was not so serious after all. I was about to thank the nice doctor for taking time out of his busy day to chat with me. Still somewhat confused by the news, I wondered if the doctor had gotten the wrong test results. Some poor man with a brain aneurysm would not know about his fate.

I asked Dr. Lucas if there was anything else I needed to do in case the dizziness returned. He said, "Dizziness is minor and not the problem to focus on right now." Sensing that shock had dulled my senses, he added with a more forceful voice, "Allen, this is serious. You have to take care of it!" He gave me the name of Dr. Nussbaum, an expert neurosurgeon, to call for further testing.

"I'll call Dr. Nussbaum's office and make an appointment," I told him. I could hear Dr. Lucas sigh on the other end.

I placed the receiver back in its cradle and stared at the deep blue, cloudless sky. The swooping seagulls were gone. Minutes passed until I realized I needed to pull myself together and get some air.

I staggered down the hall toward the elevator. As if my body and mind were no longer connected, I slumped to the floor and wrapped my arms around my knees. The barren hallway with its subtle, printed, tan-wallpapered walls started closing in on me. All I could think of were the people I had met when I was a cop who had had brain damage caused by injuries or strokes. Many of them led miserable lives. Would my aneurysm rupture before it could be repaired? Would brain surgery leave me helpless and confused or reliant on others for daily existence? I recalled the desperate wolflike howl Leaf made whenever he was afraid. I wanted to howl too.

Images of my father began to rise to the surface. Although there were good memories of boating with him and learning photography from him, I had endured his mixture of anger and ridicule toward me. I felt that I was never all he wanted in a son. Then he'd had a massive stroke while I was serving in the Air Force. As the ambulance took him away, he whispered to my mother, "I'm not even fifty."

For years he lived on as a severely disabled invalid in chronic pain. He needed constant care, and his anger erupted over no longer being independent. I felt sorry for him but also recoiled from his rage.

When his death neared, almost a decade later, Linda and I stood next to his hospital bed and witnessed the end of a shriveled and barely conscious man with a brain that had limited function.

Would I end up like my father? Would I become an invalid and resent having to be taken care of?

I bowed my head, covered my face with both hands, and acknowledged that my life as I knew it had ended. My body, my brain, my good health had failed me. Furious at my brain, I could never trust it to work right again. I looked at my right hand. It trembled slightly, as my father's had after his stroke. I began to chastise myself for being a wimp. For giving such a dramatic display in the hallway at work. I heard the elevator approaching. I'd have to pull myself up off the carpet. No one should see me like this.

Chapter Two

Meeting Harley

Seven months earlier Linda and I had been going through another ordeal: the loss of our beloved yellow Labrador retriever, Taylor. We missed hearing her paws padding along the sidewalk beside us and her tags rhythmically jingling as she trotted up and down the stairs. How I longed to have Taylor crawl like a seventy-five-pound infant onto my lap, press her head against my chest, and listen to my heartbeat. Always secure in the love of our family, she insisted on snuggling and being touched.

After the sights, sounds, and smells of Taylor faded from our home, we tentatively began discussing whether we were ready to adopt a new dog. The thought of having fur pressed against my skin once again and playful eyes pleading for me to toss a ball in the air made my heart leap with childlike expectancy. However, this anticipation was dampened by the dread of facing another loss. Dogs, with their much shorter life spans, die far too soon. I didn't know if I could ever let myself love so fully again. Rudyard Kipling said it well: "Brothers and Sisters, I bid you beware / of giving your heart to a dog to tear."

I didn't really want *another* dog. I wanted *Taylor*. She adored me. In her worldview I could do no wrong. Her devotion gleamed with purity, simplicity, and completeness. At times, when I needed to rest and relax from my days of travel, clients, and stress, it felt as if she was the only friend who made no demands on me and had no expectations.

After Taylor died I had come to a standstill. I missed the deep connection I felt with a dog who loved me unconditionally. But always, my next thought was to remember how devastating it is when that love goes away.

Loss had become an unwelcome presence in my personal life and writing career. During the months before and after Taylor's death, Linda and I had written our most difficult book to date. In it we explored the subject of animal rescue. A large portion of our book focused on the tragic losses when Hurricane Katrina bore down upon the Gulf Coast.

Because it was the fifth time that year weary residents had been urged to evacuate, many believed they would be gone for a few days, return to clean up the storm's mess, and resume life as usual. Thousands of people, with few pet-friendly hotels or homes to welcome them, had left food and water out for pets inside their homes or tethered outdoor dogs to doghouses. Consequently, the devastating hurricane had precipitated the largest animal-rescue operation in history. An estimated ten thousand volunteers and animal welfare agencies rushed to the Gulf Coast to save hundreds of thousands of pets and farm animals.

I would never be the same after chronicling the experiences and plights of good people who had endured emotional, physical, and financial pain. I admired and was inspired by those I interviewed. Talking to animal rescuers put me in the company of noble people who left their homes to save animals on the Gulf Coast, where civil unrest was the rule instead of the exception. They risked their lives and financial well-being and suffered personal losses in order to be there for the animals and their fellow human beings.

Linda and I were determined that our book would pay tribute to the sacrifices so many animal rescuers had made. There had been little recognition or praise for those who went to the front lines of a devastated area when everyone else was fleeing it. We also had a goal of compiling information and lessons learned that would prepare everyone for preventing such massive tragedies again.

While I was working on this book, I often pondered the question, "Do dogs make us better people?" After talking with rescuers and Gulf Coast residents who had waded through flooded streets, searched disease-filled houses, camped on parking lots in unsafe conditions, and spent hours on the Internet frantically trying to reunite pets who had been separated from their families, I knew the answer was a resounding "yes."

—~—

Thoughts of Taylor and other families who had lost their beloved pets were uppermost in my mind on a crisp autumn day as Linda and I found our car heading toward a local animal shelter—just to *look* at the rescued dogs. I drove past oak and maple trees that released their multicolored leaves to carpet the stiffening cold ground. Dry, cool air, a royal-blue sky, and sunshine conspired to create a perfect day.

After Linda and I arrived at the animal shelter, I noticed that little had changed since we both volunteered there years earlier. The lobby was a mix of shelves, bins, and displays of retail pet supplies. A long, high counter dominated the entry area. Shelter staff assisted people with adoptions and pet supply purchases. Posters that hung in the background behind the counter showed images of adorable dogs and cats. They served as reminders of how joyful life would become if only people adopted the charming animals and gave them "forever homes."

Volunteers from all walks of life waited eagerly to escort would-be adopters to visit with rescued dogs, cats, rabbits, and birds. Because we were familiar with the adoption routine and layout of the facility, Linda and I headed on our own toward the section that housed the adult dogs. Nothing had changed. I took in the familiar tiled walls, dividers, and heavily wired fences and gate in the dog area as well as the chain-link fencing.

I began to walk down the middle row of dogs. They barked or cowered in cages on both sides of the aisle. We asked a volunteer if we could spend time with two different dogs. When I tried to throw a ball for a little retriever, he ran to the volunteer for a hug and seemed to only have eyes for her. The other dog we asked to see, a terrier mix, cowered at the end of the dog run and trembled if I approached her. I felt sorry for the dogs but was secretly relieved. The universe might be telling us it was too soon to adopt a new dog.

After we returned to the kennel for one more look around, out of the corner of my eye I glimpsed an ink spot of fur in an adjacent row. Distracted by alarm calls from energetic, confused dogs and trying to escape the innocent desperation telegraphed in their eyes, I found it easy to ignore the tiny, furry black ball.

But Linda had noticed him too. I winced when she asked me, "Did you see that little rolled-up piece of carpet over there?" By the time we walked to the dog's kennel near the front door, the little guy was gone. "Guess someone wants to adopt him," I said. I joined Linda at the dog's empty cage and read his information card. In bold print it said: ABANDONED.

As we started to walk away to look at other dogs, a middle-aged volunteer dog-walker returned the black cocker spaniel to his cage. Linda's face immediately lit up. I felt my stomach clench. I wasn't in any shape emotionally or mentally for the full-time commitment of raising a rescued dog.

At Linda's urging I joined her to come closer to the dog who had captured her attention. His shiny, ebony coat had been groomed into the standard cocker style. The short, thick fur on his upper torso flowered into a mass of longer curls on his lower body, legs, and long ears. I whispered to Linda, "How do you think such a cute dog wound up in an animal shelter?"

I found myself focusing on the dog's face. The curve of his snout ended in an upturned nose and the widest, blackest, gleaming canine eyes I'd ever seen. He had an innocent expression that made him extremely huggable. This dog and my wife were making an instantaneous connection. My mind scrambled to organize reasons for caution.

Linda gazed into the pup's intelligent face and asked, "Do you want to come home with us?"

To my relief, the dog didn't leap into my wife's arms. Instead, he studied her face as if to say, *I'll think about it.* Abandoned as this little guy had been, it made a lot of sense for him to be wary of entrusting his fate to humans.

Another volunteer, an amiable woman of about sixty with a name tag pinned to her navy blue apron, asked, "Would you like to know more about Harley?" Linda nodded. I stood in the background, secretly waiting for this speed date to end. I wanted to get out of there before we made a disastrous mistake.

The volunteer gazed fondly at the dog as she filled us in on his scanty history. The shelter had expanded its reach by annexing other suburban community animal shelters, which were now operating as satellites. A security camera at one of the shelter's satellites had recorded a man and woman riding into the parking lot on a Harley-Davidson motorcycle and leaving a little cocker spaniel and another dog at the overnight drop-off area. The facility was closed, so the staff had no background information on the orphans. The intake person named the cocker spaniel Harley because of the vehicle that had brought him to the shelter.

Before Harley left the satellite shelter, he was neutered. After recovering from surgery, he'd been placed on the kennel floor for a week. When no one adopted him, the staff decided that he might have a better chance of finding a home if he were sent to the main shelter.

"How about a private visit with Harley?" the volunteer asked. Without waiting for our answer, she expertly lassoed a blue leash around the dog's neck. Within minutes Linda, the volunteer, Harley, and I entered a small room about the size of a walk-in closet. A wooden bench faced a glass window overlooking the hallway. This quieter environment was supposed to help people get to know an animal better, away from barking dogs and wandering onlookers.

I wondered how many others had taken the next step of bringing Harley to one of these private rooms but had decided not to adopt him. As I observed this hyper, scattered ball of energy hop around like a rabbit, I noticed a couple of kids walking past. They stopped to press their faces against the window and watch "our dog." Yes, for a split second I felt possessive, even protective, of Harley.

From what I could tell, though, the feeling wasn't mutual. Harley's stump of a tail whirled as he stretched and hurled his tiny body against the windowpane in an attempt to play with the children. "Do you think he wants to be with a family that has kids?" Linda asked the volunteer. "He's just excited," the gray-haired woman assured her.

Harley essentially took no notice of me. I thought about the clinging, somewhat needy Taylor. I'd resolved that if we ever adopted another dog, it would be good to find one who was less attached to me. I had been Taylor's world. Her total devotion was reassuring when I needed a creature to adore me. (Wives don't quite fill that requirement.) But by being "my dog," Taylor's happiness also became my responsibility.

Harley's initial reaction to us indicated that this dog was an individual. He did not throw himself at any person who came along. I had no doubt that the process of evaluating whether or not we were good matches for each other was a two-way street. Determined to take my time, I quietly sat and watched the dog's actions and reactions. What would he do next?

Linda started talking softly to Harley. He gradually allowed her to gently run her hand along his back. The volunteer, as if reminding us of what a find this little guy was, said, "He is so cute. We think he's about a year old." To me, he looked fragile, small, and a lot younger than the shelter staff's estimate.

Was I projecting my own broken heart onto this dog? It must have been devastating to be snatched away from everything and everyone he'd ever known. All the people, sights, sounds, and familiar surroundings of his first year of life had suddenly vanished.

I sat rigidly on the bench, watching Linda talk soothingly to the dog. "Aren't you going to pet him?" she asked. The thought of touching Harley made me feel I was being disloyal to Taylor. Tentatively I reached down and carefully stroked the dog's back. Harley's body stiffened. In the next instant, he relaxed a little into my fingertips. The change was subtle. But I sensed that with the gentleness of my stroking from his forehead down his spine, something had shifted in him—and in me. Moving my hand along the pup's sleek body, I felt our first spiritual connection as a hard lump of fear dissolved.

Harley was different from any dog I'd ever had in my life. All my other dogs were female. During our marriage neither of the two dogs Linda and I had brought into our home was older. Raised from puppyhood and knowing nothing but love, they had easily become secure pet family members. Harley was also much smaller than my other large-breed dogs. With the hope that perhaps two lonely souls had met in the journey of life, I gave myself permission to look forward to a new adventure with a new friend.

The volunteer must have sensed a shift in my emotions. She said, "He's a purebred cocker spaniel. He might be gone by tomorrow. You could put Harley on a twenty-four-hour hold. That way, no one would adopt him while you're making a decision."

Linda grinned at her. "We need to go home and talk this over with the cats and the bird."

The volunteer smiled as she walked Harley back to his kennel. She might have thought my wife had been joking, but I knew that Linda was serious. The cats and the bird would have much to say about bringing home a new canine brother. I too thought a family meeting would be a considerate thing to do. Like many people who have pets, I talk to them and am surprised at times by how much they seem to understand. But I don't consider myself someone who can communicate with other people's animals.

"It's good that we're taking our time," I told Linda as I drove us home. We were doing the adult thing by placing Harley on hold and having a family meeting. Although we were delaying the decision, I detected an underlying optimism in myself that I had not felt for some time.

A half hour later Linda and I sat on our living room couch to have a chat with our cats, Cuddles and Speedy, plus Sunshine, our cockatiel, about bringing home a rescued dog we had only just met. I was still questioning if we would be up to the challenge of taking in a dog who probably required a lot of time and attention. Ahead of us lay more heavy promotion of our new book that would require interviews and travel. How would Harley adjust to reporters who wanted to visit us at home? Would he be as friendly as Taylor, Cuddles, and Sunshine had been or would he be reclusive like Speedy?

To the best of our abilities, we told Cuddles and Speedy about the black cocker spaniel who had captured our hearts so quickly. We explained that in spite of misgivings about taking on the responsibility of a year-old shelter dog who might have issues and needs, there was something endearing about the little fellow. Unlike other dogs, he did not avert his gaze when a person looked directly at him. His eyes conveyed a strong spark of intellect and perceptiveness mixed with longing. We were smitten. We were foolishly in love at first sight.

Sunshine listened to our one-sided conversation from his perch in his birdcage, occasionally adding a chirp or two. Taylor had been the family's protector with her imposing body and loud bark. All Sunshine could do was screech in alarm. All the cats could do was meow. The cats had even curled up and slept with Taylor. We once found Cuddles wedged underneath Taylor's large, warm body. Wouldn't they like to have a dog to make them all feel safer?

Probably because we so wanted to believe it, we got the impression that everyone was OK with the idea. Linda had tears in her eyes. We knew what we had to do. "I don't want to leave Harley at the animal shelter one more night," she said.

"Let's go get him," I agreed.

CHAPTER THREE

Going Home

As much as I might agree with anyone who says that we impulsively adopted a year-old rescued dog we had only met a few hours ago, I have to plead not guilty by reason of pet lover insanity. I know people who carefully think through the decision to adopt, search the Internet, and spend time at different shelters to bring home the right animal. I applaud them for it. We are well educated and have been around a multitude of dogs without being tempted. Yet we could not bring ourselves to pass on Harley even though we'd done none of the reasonable research. Go figure.

I have heard from and know people who adopted older shelter dogs, and after a brief period of adjustment, the animals blended well into their homes. For some animals, the transition from shelter to home has been instantaneous.

To help us understand Harley better, after we adopted him we started to investigate information about cocker spaniels. We found disturbing items like "cocker rage" (a genetic tendency, caused by overbreeding, in which some cocker spaniels, later in life, suddenly bite the hands that feed them) and "needs to be brushed and groomed daily" (not a good fit for our busy lifestyles). I wondered if we'd have chosen this breed had we done our homework.

For any other major decision, we'd have at least slept on it overnight. Misgivings about what we were getting into might have come had we waited for a good night's sleep to slow us down. I'm not saying anybody else should follow our example. I'm just admitting that we weren't prudent or deliberate.

After meeting Harley and feeling his pleading eyes bore into me, there was only one thing I believed we could do in good conscience. With our emotions ruling the day, we wouldn't let the homeless little fellow spend any more time in the animal shelter kennel.

Linda and I rushed back to the shelter. A string of green lights whisked us through traffic, and we arrived twenty minutes before the place closed. The adoption counter was open. Harley's papers to put him on hold still sat there, ready to be processed.

While I submitted the paperwork requesting to adopt Harley, a young clerk told me that the dog was physically in excellent shape. Later, Linda confided in me about her conviction that this dog would be a special gift from heaven. "While you signed the papers," she said, "on the inner screen of my mind, I could see a shaft of brilliant white light. It swirled in a circle around our heads. Then the light slowly entered us like a stream of water being absorbed into a river. A strong wave of divine love surged through my body with such force that I felt a jolt. I understood in that moment, this soul had joined our family."

After we completed the adoption process, Linda and I put Harley's new matching blue collar and leash on him. We brought the nervous and excited little dog to a grassy area outside the shelter. I walked him around for a few minutes so he could relieve himself, while Linda sat on a bench and watched.

A thin, tall woman with curly dark hair approached me. "Did you just adopt this dog?" she asked. After I nodded yes, she stood in front of Harley. She lowered and then raised her cupped hand toward her chest in the dog-obedience hand signal that goes with the command "sit." Trainers use this gesture because even with no training, a dog will automatically sit while raising his eyes to the treat hovering above his head. Harley immediately plopped his little butt down on the grass and stared at her. He waited for her hand to reveal a hidden treat. "Smart dog," she said.

"Smart dog," I agreed. It pleased me that someone had noticed Harley was a smart dog even before we drove off the shelter parking lot.

I gestured for him to hop into the backseat of our car. Nimbly he jumped up as if he wanted out of there as soon as possible. While I drove, Harley surveyed traffic from the side windows. His innate curiosity seemed to be overcoming a natural nervousness at being uprooted once more.

Linda said, "Let's take him for a walk around Lake Harriet before we go to the pet store."

Lake Harriet, with its Victorian pavilions and public paved trail, is a Minneapolis landmark. I felt a tinge of sadness at Linda's suggestion. The three-and-a-half-mile path around the lake had been our favorite place to walk Taylor.

After we held a memorial service for Taylor, we scattered her ashes at one of her favorite spots for viewing the lake. It seemed fitting to take Harley to Lake Harriet as a symbolic way of introducing him to our sweet friend. We had walked almost daily with Taylor, until cancer riddled her body. I sensed a visit to the lake would help to reconcile the past to the present.

When I stopped the car at a red light, a Harley-Davidson motorcycle pulled up next to us. Harley lunged from the backseat to the armrest between us. His ears flailed back. He glared at the bike and growled. Linda's eyes widened. Harley had ferociously expressed dislike for his namesake. She looked at me and said, "This dog does not want to be called Harley."

"Definitely not," I agreed.

From the shade trees around the lake, a gentle breeze swirled leaves that floated to the ground and blanketed the browning autumn grass. After we parked the car on the lake lot, Harley shot out of the backseat.

Canada geese honked, and mallard ducks quacked warnings: A new hunting dog had arrived on the scene.

Lake Harriet shone a deep blue. Sunlight sparkled off its reflecting waves. Our little cocker spaniel spied the swirling leaf piles on grassy patches alongside the path. He immediately jumped into the multicolored leaves like a little kid bouncing on a mattress.

Joy filled my heart at the sight of this dog playing. He had so much of the unknown to fear. Yet he rolled and played, and bits of pumpkin-colored leaves clung to the curly fur of his black paws.

"Harley loves leaves," I said.

Linda watched him for a while and said, "Let's call him Leaf. That name keeps coming to me. I think he'd like it." The name fit this slender dog, so light on his feet. His life had been scattered during an autumn cycle of change. "Yes, it's a perfect name," I said. "A dog named Leaf."

While watching him roll around, I decided to try out his new name. "Leaf," I called. His little head shot up, and he looked at me with the intelligent expression in his eyes that had intrigued me at the animal shelter. "Leaf," I said again, more softly this time. "Leaf."

As we continued our walk with Leaf, I began to feel lighter and less burdened. The sharp, heavy pain of Taylor's death lifted now that my heart opened with love for another being. This abandoned and confused pup desperately needed a safe and loving home with good people who would never desert him. I looked down at Leaf and inwardly proclaimed, "I'm going to be here for you from now on."

Then, as if that thought wasn't powerful enough, I said out loud, "Leaf, I'll always take care of you." I wanted him to know that he'd never go back to the animal shelter. I wish I could say that Leaf looked back at me and nodded or somehow communicated that he understood. There was no reason for him to believe that human words could be trusted. Or that promises people made to dogs would never be broken.

On the way back to the car, a large man approached us from the opposite direction. Leaf's little body stiffened. As he did when the Harley motorcycle idled next to our car, he emitted a menacing growl. Although he weighed only twenty-five pounds, I had to use my strength to pull in his leash and hold on to it tightly. Leaf acted as if he wanted to take a chunk out of the man's leg. What memory brought such a strong emotional reaction from our little cocker spaniel? I managed to stop him from lunging for the man who innocently strolled past us.

Linda and I exchanged worried glances. "OK, Leaf," I said. "It may take time for you to relax and trust us to take care of you. It's OK, boy. You will soon be home."

At the pet-supply store, Leaf smelled dog-food bags and other dogs who shopped with their people. The smiles and comments about how adorable Leaf was reassured me. We'd made the right decision by adopting such a well-adjusted, friendly rescue dog.

While nobody was looking Leaf lifted his leg to take ownership of one of the floor-level bins that contained dog treats. I caught the power play too late to stop it. While Linda held on to him, I hurried to get one of the cleanup wipes. The store supplied them for overly stimulated canine customers.

When we went to check out, the young cashier said, "I have a girl cocker spaniel. I love her so much. Do you have problems house training? I've had my dog for over a year. She still has never been house-trained. But I love her."

I thought about the smell in the clerk's home. I knew that I would work hard to teach Leaf where to go to the bathroom. Our previous two dogs had been relatively easy to train. We'd only had to take them to a spot in the backyard a few times, and they'd figured out exactly what we wanted them to do.

When we arrived home Leaf was hesitant. Unlike the eager Taylor, he didn't immediately leap from the seat. "He's cautious," I told Linda. I snapped the leash onto his collar and signaled for him to jump out of the car. "OK, boy," I encouraged. He bounded onto the concrete garage floor. Was he starting to trust me already?

We walked through the backyard and into the back door of our home. Leaf thrust his nose in the air and took a long, slow inhale of the world he was about to enter. "Cats," Linda crooned. We laughed. The smart cats were nowhere in sight. They were most likely downstairs in their "basement apartment."

I snapped off Leaf's leash. He hurried into the kitchen. Feverishly he sniffed everything. When we entered the dining room from the kitchen, his paws touched the carpeted floor. He yanked his right paw back as if he'd had an electrical shock. The carpet with its multiple odors—cat, human, Taylor—must have unnerved him. Linda said, "It looks like he's never walked on carpet before."

"Maybe he hasn't been inside a house," I added.

Leaf made his way from the dining room into the living room. He glanced at me from the corners of his eyes and did another quick inhale with his upturned nose. The depth of his sniffing told me that with each step he cataloged all the rich new scents.

Linda was concerned that the cats would be indignant and then angry if they didn't at least get to see their new brother. We knew the importance of gradually introducing a new pet into the home. The older residents have to first become accustomed to the smells and sights of an unfamiliar animal.

I went downstairs, picked up our seven-pound, black-and-white tuxedo cat Cuddles, and held her in my arms. Raised as a kitten and adopted from the same animal shelter where we'd found Leaf, Cuddles is our self-appointed hostess. When reporters come to the house to interview us about our books, Cuddles wins them over by playfully posing for the camera.

While Linda held on to Leaf, I stood at a distance and showed him to Cuddles. She reared up her spine and hissed at him. Leaf playfully lunged toward her, and she spat back at him. "Enough of that," Linda said. "She knows he's here."

I took Cuddles back downstairs and placed her on the soft pillow of her couch. She glared at me. If Cuddles, our friendly cat, had had such a reaction, what would happen with Speedy, our skittish tabby? He was not at all fond of strangers. Still, I thought it was important for Speedy to get his own sniff of the intruder. His green eyes glowered at the bouncing dog. Within seconds I returned Speedy to his basement couch. If it were up to him, I'm sure he'd just as soon never again lay eyes on that dog.

Linda and I sat on the couch to think about what to do next. I said, "Guess Leaf doesn't exactly remind the cats of Taylor." While we talked, Leaf found the picture window that spans the living room wall and overlooks the city sidewalk in front of our house. He hunched down on his back legs. His tiny face landed at exactly the right height for peering over the windowpane. Occasionally his tail wagged as a person walking a dog passed by the house.

The bird on his perch remained uncharacteristically quiet. If he had yearned for more drama to keep him entertained, his wish had come true. Sunshine's head bobbed from side to side. He watched Leaf dart from one room to another. Any noise or sound caught the dog's attention, and he'd run toward it.

For some reason Leaf's nervousness and discomfort made my affection for him grow. I assumed that for some period of time, he'd had to take care of himself. He looked like a pup who learned not to rely on others. Yet I sensed that this dog needed me.

After a few days the cats could come upstairs. They'd go back to their routine of looking out the living room window and lounging on their carpeted kitty condo. We planned to put up a gate we had purchased at the pet store between the hallway and my office. Leaf could stay in one section of the house, and the cats could get used to his presence without having to be in the same room with him.

We also bought a large fabric-covered dog crate and a soft dog bed that fit into it. Leaf would have a man cave to call his own. As for crate training, we'd learn more about that careful process later when we bought a book on the subject.

On the first night of Leaf's arrival, we thought he might be scared, so we put his crate in our bedroom. That way, he'd be able to hear us breathing and feel comforted. At first he whimpered. Then, as if he was an instrument reaching crescendo pitch, Leaf's whimper turned into a howl. If anyone doubts that dogs descended from wolves, they'd only need to hear Leaf's howling to know the truth. One or two blood-curdling wails prompted Linda to wish hopefully, "He'll stop in a few minutes." Ten minutes later he was still baying.

We tried to calm him. I found a night-light and plugged it in, so that its glow warmed the bedroom. Again, we switched off our bedside lamps. The howling resumed.

"Leaf, what's wrong, baby?" Linda asked.

Five more minutes of shrieking. Then Leaf became quiet. We almost fell asleep when Leaf started yowling as if announcing the end of the world. I moved his dog bed out of the crate and placed it closer to our bed.

"He might need to go outside," I told Linda after he howled again. I put on my clothes and fastened Leaf's leash to his collar. We trekked out the front door for a midnight stroll. He walked around in circles in the front yard. We hadn't yet established a place for him to go regularly in the backyard. No scents were sweet enough to signal his spot. Finally he peed a little. Could sleep be in sight?

I trundled him back indoors. He sniffed the carpet. Before I could stop him, he lifted his leg and left his mark. He *did* have to go after all.

Linda got up and found the pet-stain remover we'd bought that day. She soaked the wet spot with the solution. Then she sat on the living room floor and sighed.

Since we couldn't sleep, we discussed our options. We resolved to return to the pet-supply store and find an herbal remedy that could help to calm our dog's nerves. Throughout the first night I repeatedly took Leaf outside for bathroom breaks. He didn't need to go anymore. Why would he? Our living room had served as his urinal.

By morning two sleep-deprived new dog parents faced each other over a cup of strong coffee. Their rescued cocker spaniel snored quietly outside his dog crate.

CHAPTER FOUR

Leaf's Secrets

I HOPED THAT WE'D EVENTUALLY DISCOVER ENOUGH CLUES TO LEAF'S secret past for us to be able to help him heal. As I soon discovered, he brought many scars with him from his previous life. Severe separation anxiety made it difficult to ever let him be by himself, even in a room in our house. His unfamiliarity with living indoors destroyed our carpet. Due to his strong chase instinct, he terrorized our cats. Leaf lurched at other dogs, rabbits, and squirrels whenever we walked him around the neighborhood, which meant sore shoulders and knees for us.

I looked to veterinarians, trainers, and animal-loving friends for help. Because animal communicators had helped us with our pets in the past, I was grateful when one of them offered to listen to Leaf telepathically.

Marcia Wilson, a California woman who had served as a judge in our Angel Animals story contests, offered to tune in to our troubled boy. On a cold November day, Linda, Leaf, and I huddled together in a quiet bedroom to have a conversation with Marcia by phone. She quickly told us, "This is different than my sessions with other dogs. Leaf is very quiet. Too quiet. He won't talk to me."

What could we do? Although each person we consulted had given important pieces to the puzzle that was Leaf, no one had been able to adequately advise us on how to make him more comfortable or less anxious. Our sleepless nights were blending into stress-filled days as we tried to cope with all of this dog's erratic behaviors and fears.

Marcia tried to reassure Leaf. "All your new mom and dad want to do is to make life better for you." Then she asked him what had happened at the shelter. His answer would make us understand the depth and source of his suffering.

"I got left."

When Marcia told us what Leaf had communicated to her, he lowered his head. His body slumped to the floor. Marcia, who couldn't see Leaf's body language, said, "He feels so much shame. He doesn't know what he did wrong."

Even though Linda and I reassured him that this was his forever home, would Leaf still wonder if he would ever be left again? How long would it take before he believed that no matter how often we corrected him or gave him time-outs in his comfortable crate, he was home? How much praise and affection would he require to bolster his self-esteem? Could he believe that we'd never stop loving him?

After making a revelation that obviously destroyed what little self-confidence he had, Leaf did not want to discuss it further with Marcia, as the memory was too painful. When the session ended, we tried to console him with a pat on the head, but he turned away from us. His little body quivered with embarrassment and grief.

On the first few visits Leaf and I made to the dog park, my heart ached to see him study the faces of each dog who entered the park. Not in the way dogs do when they're scouting a prospective playmate, but in the desperate way of someone who has lost a best friend. I was reminded of what the animal shelter volunteer had told us. "Harley" had been dropped off at the after-hours reception area with another dog. Had the two dogs been each other's only friends in the world? Is this the buddy Leaf looked for in every dog he met?

Since we had made progress with Marcia, we decided to try a phone session with another animal communicator named Mary Stoffel. We

wanted Mary to talk with Leaf about how he should conduct himself around cats. Mary took a few minutes to tune in telepathically to Leaf. He remained quiet with her too, at first. She communicated with him about the nature of cats. "They're nothing like dogs." Mary told Leaf that when he chased the cats, they had to defend themselves by clawing at his ears and face. They could hurt him. He'd have to leave them alone.

After Mary finished communicating with Leaf, we explained to her that in addition to his panic attacks, he became aggressive upon meeting certain types of people, such as the large white male who had walked toward him at Lake Harriet. And yet he seemed to gravitate toward men, especially Latino men.

Based on Leaf's specific fears and behaviors, Mary speculated that he might be a puppy-mill dog. I had done research on puppy mills for our animal-rescue book. Often, purebred dogs, especially popular breeds such as cocker spaniels, were sold from these horrific places to pet stores, where people bought them. The unsuspecting buyers don't realize that the pups have been treated inhumanely and might develop severe behavioral and physical problems. Animal shelters are the sad recipients of many puppy-mill/pet-store dogs. People surrender them after they wreak havoc on the buyers' homes and wallets.

Leaf certainly had some of the characteristics of a puppy-mill dog—more so than we realized at the time. Mary's theory made sense to us. After the session with her, we were grateful to notice that Leaf's cat chasing, although not over, decreased considerably.

In those early months Leaf constantly needed to be with one of us. He never wanted to lose sight of a human. He must have held to the idea that if he was always in our company, he would not be left again. He followed me from room to room. If I wasn't at home, he stayed near Linda.

When he napped, he'd often wake up disoriented. The whites of his eyes reddened, his entire body trembled, and he would hurl his head back. His eyes glazed over as if he had entered another realm. With uncontrollable fear, he'd emit ear-piercing shrieks. Even when we'd rush into the room to reassure him that he wasn't alone, he didn't recognize us and couldn't stop wailing. It took lots of soothing to calm him down.

Our neighbors told me, "We can hear your dog howling all the way over here." I wondered if they thought we might be mistreating him and explained about his separation anxiety. But they knew how much we loved animals and understood that we were dealing with something over which we had no control.

We were never quite sure how Leaf would react. Once when he started howling out of the blue, I said to him loudly, "Leaf, look around. You're home. It's normal." To my relief, he snapped out of it and wagged his tail. Then to my shock and without hesitation, he rolled over on his back and I gave him the first tummy rub that he allowed me to give. That's also when I discovered what would become Leaf's magic word: *normal*. A guy who had lost everything loved when life was normal.

Night after night Leaf's wolf howls continued to keep me on edge. At times he would come over to my side of the bed and place his front paws on the mattress. His lustrous dark eyes would look at me with desperation as I peeked at him half-asleep.

"Need to go outside?" I'd ask him softly, so as not to wake Linda. We didn't have a fenced-in backyard, so I took Leaf for as many as three walks per night, often between midnight and 4 a.m.

Winters are harsh in the Twin Cities. During the first season with Leaf, nature hit us with all its might. Subzero winds fought through my protective clothing. Inches of snow formed over layers of ice on the sidewalks. I had to bundle up in a heavy coat, hat, and gloves several times each night to serve his multiple attempts at elimination. Poor Leaf was constipated a lot, and his response to any pressure to hurry up so we could get back inside ensured that things wouldn't happen. Elimination, like every other process for this often terrified dog, had to take place on his own schedule. I soon learned the key to success was movement. If we walked at a fast pace, he was more likely to do his business. Then we could escape the windchill and go back inside. Somehow I managed not to fall on the slick sidewalks that entire winter.

Many times I did not return to bed after the first walk around the neighborhood. Instead, I'd go to my room across the hall from our bedroom and sit in my old tan recliner chair. I'd pick up Leaf, put him on my lap, and prop his head on a small blue pillow. Listening to his rapidly beating heart, I'd feel his legs twitch, as they sprawled across my chest and abdomen. "You're such a sweet pup," I'd tell him in a low voice.

In these moments Leaf would study my face as I chanted HU, a sacred word that is said to be the sound within all sounds of creation. I learned about HU through Eckankar, a spiritual teaching that has shown me how to recognize the spark of God in each person and animal I meet. Singing HU soothed my dog's anxious body and mind. His head would lower and rest on my chest. I sensed that at last, he felt safe next to a warm body and a steady human heartbeat. With a loud sigh, he'd soundly drift into a deep sleep. And so would I, for whatever remained of the dwindling nighttime hours.

How could I keep up this sleep-deprived routine? I did not know. How long would I do this? For as long as it took.

CHAPTER FIVE

Never Give Your Wife a Memo

LEAF'S NIGHTLY OUTINGS AND THE HOURS SPENT WITH HIM SLEEPING on my lap brought healing for both of us. He was bonding with me, and I was recovering from the loss of Taylor. By the time Dr. Lucas delivered the news that I had a brain aneurysm, the effects of those special moments had strengthened me emotionally. After my initial meltdown on the floor outside an elevator at my office, I was able to grant myself only a few more minutes of self-pity. I had to return to my office and try to get my act together.

I pushed my hands against the wall and managed to stand up. My mind raced as I thought, *Walk slowly. Try to understand what just happened here. Focus.* Since my reaction to the doctor's news had been so emotional, I dreaded the effect it would have on my wife.

While Linda had shown amazing strength through her own challenges with breast cancer five years earlier, she is especially sensitive to any pain of mine and of our children. If I told her my news, I feared she'd fly into a panic. Would there be uncharacteristic over-the-top drama? She might become unreasonable. What if she cried? I never knew how to handle it when she had what to me was an emotional reaction. I would tell her, "Everything will be OK." But would everything be OK this time?

I decided not to tell her. I'd convince her to visit her parents in Texas and schedule the operation while she was out of town. But if she found out I had surgery while she was gone, she'd go ballistic. *Alright,* I told myself, *she'll be upset for two or three weeks but then she'll be OK.* Then again, it could be a sore point for many years. Maybe even a lifetime.

Yes, I was having a crisis. But since facts, statistics, and options had always been my first and best resort for handling crises, I decided to make a plan. Any challenge could become manageable with rational, deliberate analysis, I reasoned. What would Spock do? This new way of viewing the news brought relief even though I was angry at my brain. How could it let me down like this? A broken brain? Seriously?

When I googled "brain aneurysm," hundreds of entries flooded the screen. There were horror stories of botched surgeries, lifelong disabilities, and blood bubbles that caused people intense suffering and pain. The more I read, the more miraculous I realized it was that mine had been found before it burst. Dr. Lucas was right. I was one of the fortunate ones.

None of these websites were going to make it easy to tell my wife about any of this. My anxiety started to rise again, so I clicked onto the

Angel Animals Network website, where I could look at photos of Leaf playing in the snow during his first winter with us. What was it about this troubled little guy that calmed me?

Suddenly an idea, a brilliant idea, came to me. My job as a computer-software analyst often required me to perform "information management" of collected data. For my wife, I'd design a fact sheet about brain aneurysms and surgery. It would include an easy-to-read overview, definitions, possible options, and most importantly, success stories. I'd leave out the horrors and unsettling statistics. It would be information *manipulation* management. The fact sheet would ease Linda into my new reality. For the first time since Dr. Lucas's call, a slight smile flitted across my face. I was taking charge.

I constructed the report with as much care and detachment as one can when talking about brain surgery. I played around with descriptive words to make it sound less serious. In a stroke of genius, I decided to refer to the operation as a "surgical procedure." I thought the lighter terminology might help Linda ease into the situation. With time, she'd adjust, and then we could have a reasonable discussion about how to proceed.

I also researched the neurosurgeon to whom Dr. Lucas referred me. Dr. Eric S. Nussbaum had impressive credentials. He had authored numerous journal articles and a book on the innovative procedure he developed for clipping brain aneurysms. I called and made the appointment. I appreciated Dr. Lucas's referral to the best neurosurgeon in the Midwest. Perhaps the best in the country.

By the time I finished the fact sheet, I proudly viewed it as a masterpiece of practical understatement. I planned to present it to Linda that night. I figured she'd read it and not give the news too much more thought.

"You're telling me you have a brain aneurysm? You're going to need brain surgery? And you gave me a memo?!" Linda shrieked at me as she glared at the fact sheet on the dining room table.

"I have an *un*ruptured brain aneurysm," I explained. "The factual information I presented was to reassure you that all could be handled within the realm of reason. And without emotional drama." I sort of choked on that last statement as I recalled my near breakdown earlier that day.

"This is not a memo situation!"

Without thinking, I said, "When I found out, I wondered if you needed to know, that maybe I would be able to . . ." I looked at her and realized it would probably be best to stop talking.

Instead, I reached out for Linda's hand. We walked into the living room and sat on the couch. There, we had an honest conversation about everything that was at stake. I told her what I remembered from the conversation with Dr. Lucas. I said I'd made an appointment with Dr. Nussbaum for an evaluation. We talked about how we would get through this—together.

I held Linda in my arms while tears filled her eyes. The no-drama idea went out the window, as it probably should have from the onset. I realized that when you have bad news, it's better to hold hands and talk about it rather than present your wife with a well-constructed, typed, and printed document.

While Linda and I discussed what could be a dismal future, Leaf stretched out on the fireplace hearthstone nearby. Mary, the animal communicator we consulted, had told us that Leaf referred to this spot as his "carved-out place." If he needed privacy to process whatever was happening in his life, his carved-out place became his personal refuge. We always respected his need for space and didn't touch or try to engage him when he retreated to the hearthstone.

Tonight, he listened to us talking with his head resting on his paws. He seemed to be taking in our emotions and pondering the situation. Even though he couldn't convey concerns in human language, I sensed he understood that a funnel cloud barreled toward our home.

What could a young pup do to avert disaster for him and the people he had come to depend upon?

Chapter Six

Memory Lane

AFTER SCHEDULING MY APPOINTMENT WITH DR. NUSSBAUM FOR a week after the phone call from Dr. Lucas, my warm feelings about the growing trust of my little ball of black fur mixed with foreboding. I recalled that shortly before Dr. Lucas's call, without warning or reason, I'd been having the strangest visual episodes. A pounding sensation would start in my forehead between my eyebrows like boulders barreling down from a mountaintop, and disturbing images would push toward the surface of my mind. I felt dumbfounded by this unstoppable visual barrage.

I was driving to the office one day when suddenly snapshots of past events appeared like images on a high-definition screen. I struggled to focus on the traffic around me. Each memory reminded me of a moment when I'd been petty, bitter, or selfish toward my family. Although I hadn't thought about these incidents in years, they now appeared to be etched on my psyche.

Some of the most disturbing memories were of arresting violent people. Movies and television dramas that depict police in action show them quickly moving from one incident to the next without much reflection. In reality, the aftermath of a horrid crime sticks in a cop's mind like poison.

I finally made it into the parking garage and slammed my car door with more force than I had intended. The mental snapshots ended as quickly as they had started.

The troubling images continued to invade my mind with varying levels of intensity over the next few weeks. Occasionally I'd have two or three days free of the attacks. But soon the memories would begin again with even more ferocity.

I knew there had to be a reason for this, but what could it be? I had done good things in my life. I'd always worked hard at each job. Why wasn't I recalling personal accomplishments? After all, I'd been a decent person—a good son, father, friend, employee, brother, and husband. And now a person who was helping a broken dog become whole again.

⁓⁓

Having all these unbidden flashes of my previous mistakes caused me to contemplate how I'd arrived at this point in my life. With Leaf soundly snoring on my chest after our nightly walks, I reflected on how single events, even ones that seemed unremarkable at the time, could change the direction of a person's life.

In Atlanta I'd been assigned to a high-crime section of the city. I answered a domestic-dispute call late one night. By the time I arrived at the apartment's ground-level entrance, the verbal battle between a man and woman was in full swing. Theirs was a classic domestic fight over money, and the use of drugs and alcohol had made it escalate.

I worked to bring the noise level down a couple of notches and calm the craziness. A young boy of about seven or eight sat on the battling couple's stained green sofa near a dimly lit lamp. Next to him cuddled a shorthaired mutt. The dog clung to the boy's side and licked tears off the dazed child's cheeks. This little dog took it upon himself to protect the boy while chaos swirled around them.

The couple's emotions eventually cooled off. Like many domestic disputes, my only recourse was to separate these two people for the night. I hoped that they would have a less threatening discussion of their differences the following day.

I took a mental snapshot of the scene of the child and his comforting dog. Observing the love between them in such an extreme circumstance caused me to think about our family's golden retriever Prana. She often restored my sanity and helped heal me after the intensity of a full watch on inner-city patrol. After one especially rough night-watch in Atlanta, I came home exhausted. Linda and the kids were sleeping, and I didn't want to wake them. Still in uniform, with my gun belt on, I slowly dropped my weary body onto the carpeted floor. Prana sidled next to me. She pressed herself hard against my side. I looked over to see her gently licking my hand. Without taking her eyes off me, she started caressing my cheek with her soft tongue. I felt all the stress and emotions of that night slowly dissipate. It was as if Prana soaked up all the negativity and took away my burdens. She gave without asking anything in return.

Police work was convincing me that people were rarely good at finding safety and love with one another. But that night with the little boy and dog, something inside switched. I decided that I wanted to write about how animals brought unconditional love, healing, and security to people when they needed it most.

Now, this wish was being fulfilled in my work with Linda. I remembered that afternoon years ago when she and I talked about the next stage of our lives as we walked Taylor around Lake Harriet.

"Animals really are like angels," Linda commented. I watched a lone, white seagull fly near the water's edge.

"We're not alone in how strongly we feel about our pets," I said. "Think how empty and quiet our home would be without the gang there."

"We both love to write and we love animals," Linda said with a grin. "What if we combined the two things?"

"Are enough people interested in that kind of writing?"

Many people I knew thought of their pets as disposable property. I wondered if there were others who observed and believed in the spiritual nature of animals as sentient beings.

Linda suggested that we help ordinary people express their appreciation for animal heroes in everyday life. Taking a deep breath, Linda looked at me and said, "Since we want to bring out the spiritual element in animals, let's call our writing 'Angel Animals.'"

A few months later, we were calling ourselves the Angel Animals Network. We started publishing true stories from around the world in our homegrown, subscription-based Angel Animals Newsletter. Within a year we were doing fund-raisers for local animal shelters, were featured on local TV and in newspapers, and were having articles about us picked up by national wire services. We had more than a thousand subscribers

to our newsletter, wrote a proposal for our first book, acquired a literary agent, and signed a contract for Angel Animals, the book. One book grew into dozens more.

Minnesota turned out to be the best spot on earth for launching a project that focused on books about animals and the nice people who love them. It was the land of ducks, geese, and innocence. Being polite, known as "Minnesota Nice," seemed to be number one on the list of requirements for living here. A four-way stop at an intersection took forever to get through. Nobody wanted to be overly presumptuous or appear rude by going first. Instead, without any honking, drivers waved for others to proceed until someone finally moved. For the first time in my life, I saw traffic on a busy four-lane highway stop both ways while drivers patiently waited for a family of mallard ducks to waddle across the highway.

Before we had even made the decision to move from Atlanta, on our first visit to Minneapolis and St. Paul, Linda pointed to graffiti scrawled on the underpass of a concrete bridge wall. "All the words are correctly spelled and punctuated," she said. When my face didn't register the humor in her statement, she continued, "They take education seriously in Minnesota."

At fast-food restaurants, clean-cut servers spoke intelligently and appeared to have been transported from jobs at Disneyland. Minnesota had one of the highest literacy rates and number of people finishing high school. When a teenage server at a coffee shop asked, "Would you like cutlery with your muffin?" I knew we were home.

Now, on the nights prior to my appointment with the brain surgeon, I sat with Leaf's relaxed body spread across my knees. I did not yet know how Leaf would transform from an emotionally needy pup into a fiercely courageous healer in my future. I wondered if the upsetting flashbacks to my past mistakes and regrets were serving as preludes to the treacherous course my life was about to take.

Although my strong faith would strengthen my connection with family, friends, and coworkers, ultimately, no matter how much they loved me, there would be a time when no one could give me the assurance I needed. I would have to rely on the help of a slender, floppy-eared dog. He would be the heavenly messenger to save my life as surely as if he had swum out into the ocean and pulled my drowning body to shore.

PART TWO

Nightmares, Battles, and Surrender

One ship drives east and another drives west
With the selfsame winds that blow
'Tis the set of the sails
And not the gales
Which tells us the way to go.
                    —ELLA WHEELER WILCOX, "THE WINDS OF FATE"

CHAPTER SEVEN

Doctor Doogie Howser

THE DAY OF MY APPOINTMENT WITH DR. NUSSBAUM ARRIVED TOO quickly. I'd soon have to make decisions that would affect everything. I have a high regard for the brain, particularly *my* brain. My primary fear was that if the aneurysm burst before or during surgery, I would become disabled. I worried I would become like my father—a burden on others. How could I keep my job if my memory and problem-solving functions were reduced or destroyed altogether?

Dr. Nussbaum's Minneapolis office was located in a green-tinted, glass-encased, seven-story building near Lake Harriet. How ironic, I thought, that Linda, Leaf, Taylor, and I had blithely walked around the Minneapolis lakes countless times over the years, passing the building where my brain surgeon had his office. Was this some kind of cosmic joke? The building had what appeared to be a metal sailboat perched on its roof, as if steering the building into a lake headwind. Even though sailboats dotted the lake each summer season, the artsy version of a sailboat looked out of place to me.

With so much out of my hands, I worked to keep some aspects of life under my control, including knowing where I would be going for an important appointment. I decided to scout out the doctor's office the day before our visit was scheduled. Upon arrival I found that the building's signage only contained the name of the neurosurgery center, not the doctor's name.

The following day I dropped off Leaf at his doggie day-care center. At least I had the assurance that he'd be looked after while we were at an appointment to determine my future.

Linda and I slowly walked toward the building's side door. I took a quick look at the familiar city lake. How I wished to be walking around its choppy blue water on this gray day with my pup light on his feet and not a care in the world.

The moment we entered the ground floor of the building, I smelled fresh coffee and muffins wafting from the coffee shop.

"Muffins?" I asked, trying to tempt Linda.

"Maybe on our way out," she replied unenthusiastically.

Normally I would have a tough time passing up such a treat. But today, we reluctantly continued our trek, with me leading the way.

Linda became quieter. I needed to give her some space.

As I pushed the elevator button to the floor for Dr. Nussbaum's office, anger rose like bile in my throat. I wanted to blurt out, "What am I doing here? This is all a mistake!" My next thought was *where is all the emotion coming from? What happened to my reasonable, Spock-like approach to the situation?* The elevator door opened, and we entered—one quiet and one very angry person.

The hallway outside the doctor's fourth-floor office was under construction. Large plastic sheets lined the halls, and floors exposed bare concrete. No one was working, although unsettled sawdust swirled in the sunlit air. I had noticed construction materials and the stripped-down floor on my scouting mission the day before but was still taken aback at having to make my way through it now. Was this a sign of what I'd find inside? Sloppiness, unfinished business, poor attention to detail?

I opened the door to Dr. Nussbaum's office and let Linda enter first. I almost closed the door behind her. Couldn't I just stay in the safety of the hallway? Couldn't I wait out in the car while she talked to the doctor?

The young receptionist was businesslike and expressionless. She handed me a clipboard and asked me to fill out a form for gathering basic background information. Linda and I found two empty chairs together and sat down. I quickly filled out the form and returned it to the receptionist. I looked over at Linda. Her eyes telegraphed that she felt frightened. We usually chatted about almost everything. But now we sat in silence, taking in the sights and sounds of the office lobby.

When I'm feeling nervous in a new situation, I sometimes take my mind off what I'm about to do by mentally redecorating the environment. The first thing I noticed in the reception area was its nearly naked walls and sparse furniture. I imagined adding a few paintings of dogs, cats, and nature scenes. While indulging in this game didn't make me feel better about being there, it allowed me not to immediately focus on the unnerving details of other patients in the room.

When I did let myself observe the people around me, I noticed that some wore baseball caps or head coverings. Others showed long scars across their skulls. The sight of shaved or bald heads, visible wounds, and the sounds of whispered speech forced me to remember why I was there.

I looked at Linda and touched her hand. She shared a nervous smile and handed me a brochure about Dr. Nussbaum that she picked up from the reception desk. I had done some initial research, but this brochure made it clearer that the man who would hold my life in his hands was more famous in the world of brain surgery than we knew.

He was recognized worldwide for being an expert in a highly effective procedure for closing off blood flow in the brain. It involved the traditional clipping of the artery that feeds the aneurysm, thereby eliminating the risk of a rupture. He had done so many of these procedures that he was considered the best. His book on the subject was in bookstores. An entire wing of a hospital was dedicated to his neurosurgery patients.

I felt better after reading the brochure, but it gave birth to new worry. My research had indicated that there were two ways to go with brain-aneurysm surgery. One would be to have invasive surgery with clipping. The other alternative was a less invasive procedure of intravascular entry and then filling the aneurysm from the inside with material that would block blood from entering the area.

I wanted to make sure that after the doctor had answered my questions about the two options, I stayed neutral about which type of surgery to choose. My decision needed to be based on facts and not an emotional preference. I did not want to build a case in my mind for one procedure over the other. I just wanted the facts.

I clutched the large brown envelope containing images of the X-ray CAT scan that Dr. Nussbaum's superefficient nurse Jody Lowary had told me to bring to the office for my first visit. "It is all in here," I said to Linda as I held up the envelope. It was a bit surreal that the package contained brain images that could determine my destiny.

A cheerful woman in her late fifties, wearing a colorful-print medical smock, walked out to the waiting room and loudly called, "Allen Anderson."

I would have preferred that she call me "Mr. Anderson" so the world, which at the time was everyone in the waiting room, would not know such personal information as my first name. I still clung to the idea that the diagnosis was a mistake, a misunderstanding, and I didn't belong here anyway.

In the consultation room I carefully examined the large chart on the wall. It displayed well-rendered drawings. They depicted perfectly formed red and gray unruptured aneurysms ballooning from arteries. Each aneurysm had a well-defined neck. I wondered if mine looked that way. If I could have one request in this experience, I wanted my aneurysm to have a well-defined neck. It would be easier for the doctor to clip and make the less invasive surgery an option.

When the esteemed doctor entered the office, I kept my facial expression neutral so it wouldn't register surprise. He introduced himself, turned away from me, and took a seat behind his desk. While he had his back to us, I looked at Linda. She mouthed words, but I couldn't make out what she said. Later she told me that on first seeing Dr. Nussbaum, all she could think of was the fictional television character Dr. Doogie Howser—a sixteen-year-old brilliant physician who works as a hospital resident.

I stared at Dr. Nussbaum's hands, thinking about the requirements for his profession. I reassured myself that younger people tend to have steadier hands. In this respect, surely his youth would be a plus while doing delicate brain surgery.

Nurse Jody joined us in the office. Dr. Nussbaum pulled out the CAT scan images to view. I briefly wondered if Nurse Jody played Dr. Watson to his Sherlock Holmes. Holmes was the mastermind of any mystery. In an effort to cheer myself up, I decided that Holmes would be my nickname for Dr. Nussbaum.

The doctor patiently answered each of the questions from a list I'd prepared. When I asked, "Which side of the brain will you enter?" he looked surprised at the question. He evaluated the CAT scan again and told me he would open my skull on the right side. "Check. Drill right side of brain," I wrote on my list.

I glanced over at Linda. Her eyes had glazed over. She sat with lips frozen in a grim line. Her hands clasped together tightly in her lap.

Dr. Nussbaum posted the CAT scan on the wall so we could all look at it. An unfocused blob lay where only an artery should be. It looked nothing like the nice, easy-to-see, colorful drawings on his office wall chart. "I don't see a well-defined neck to the aneurysm," he said.

Disappointment slapped me in the face. The surgeon was not giving me the answer I wanted to my one request.

"I need for you to have an arteriogram." He explained that the test would provide a more detailed picture of my brain.

"If an aneurysm does not have a well-defined neck, is it harder to clip?" I asked.

"I can clip anything," he answered with confidence.

I was beginning to like this guy.

CHAPTER EIGHT

Leaf at Home

OUR HOME LIFE HAD CHANGED FROM PEACEFUL ROUTINE TO BEDLAM UPON Leaf's four-pawed entry into it. Only seven months after our troubled dog's arrival, my future had now become uncertain. Simultaneously, we were boxers dodging flailing fists that threatened to knock us both down for the count.

One of the few routine pleasures Linda and I continued was to take occasional breaks and visit our favorite coffee shop. Before Leaf (BL) we often went there to write, plan, and reflect on our projects. A little caffeine made us feel as if we could accomplish any goal. While sipping lattés and watching local residents walk their dogs past the shop, we relaxed by discussing books we were reading, movies we wanted to see, and other creative endeavors.

Our discussion topics dramatically changed after Leaf (AL). These conversations usually went something like this, with comments neither of us could believe we were making in public:

Linda: "Did he poop?"

Me: "Uh?"

Linda: "Did he poop? We have to get him house-trained."

Me: "Yes, yes, he did go."

Linda: "Both ways?"

Me: "Pooped and peed. He is empty."

Linda: "Was it firm?"

Me: "Uh-hum."

Linda: "How firm?"

Me: "Real hard!"

Our concerns over Leaf's bowel movements dominated our conversations during those days. Leaf's initial constipation had turned into bouts of diarrhea. We'd have to take him to the veterinarian if we couldn't figure out how to make him regular, and another vet visit was not something I wanted to put Leaf or us through. The first time we took him to the Westgate Pet Clinic office, only a few days after adopting him, we were worried to see kindly Dr. Bennett Porter muzzle him and write "aggressive" in our new dog's medical record. At the end of the exam, Leaf wagged his tail and took treats from Dr. Porter's hand. He said, "That's a good sign. He's not a mean dog." I felt relieved.

Leaf had been terrified when Dr. Porter administered shots and patted him up and down his body. He seemed to believe he was alone and had to fend for himself again. Even though we were with him in the room, where he could see us, we hadn't proven to him yet that we were trustworthy protectors.

Leaf's multitude of issues also changed the way we did media interviews. As featured guests on radio shows for our new book, we had to convey deep feelings around the heartfelt topic of animal rescue. The true stories we told often moved hosts, listeners, and guests alike.

The media interviews were successful and painless if we were prepared, focused, and ready to field unexpected questions. We usually did what is called a "phoner"—an interview that isn't at a studio or in person with a journalist but happens over the telephone. During phoners it's important that the environment be free of distractions and noise. Linda and I would sit at separate tables and signal to each other about who should answer the host's or reporter's questions. At least, that's how phoners worked BL. AL it was a different story.

"I don't know if Leaf will stay quiet," I said while I set up the two phones for one interview.

"He'll sleep," Linda said hopefully.

"There are five more interviews in the next week. We have to figure out how to do them with Leaf here."

If we isolated Leaf where he couldn't see us in the house, his howls would unnerve us and wreck the interview. The radio host and station engineers, plus listeners, would hear our poor suffering dog yelling for help. From experience, we knew that once Leaf's crying started, it didn't stop until he assured himself that he wasn't alone. Sometimes it took a few minutes for him to calm down. On air that amount of time would seem like an eternity.

"OK," I said, "we'll keep him in the room with us. We'll give him a toy and a bone to chew." Secretly I was remembering how Taylor quietly slept under the table while we did phoners. She didn't even snore, as Leaf did with his doggy sleep apnea.

We settled Leaf with a toy just as the phone rang. I answered, and Linda picked up the extension. The host introduced us to her audience. We were on the air live. This was Leaf's cue to transform into a whirlwind of activity.

Like a toddler whose parents have averted their attention and given him free reign to open kitchen cabinets or empty wastebaskets, Leaf seized his opportunity. I answered questions with one hand while trying to hold him in place. My voice rose from normal to high pitch and then to a level only dogs could hear. Leaf slipped out of my grasp.

When it was Linda's turn to answer a serious question about how many animals had been rescued after Hurricane Katrina, Leaf jumped on the couch. He ran across the end table and unsettled a large lamp. I put my phone down as quietly as possible and managed to catch the lamp before it crashed to the floor.

As I precariously held the lamp with my left hand and grabbed for the phone receiver with my right hand to hear the host's next question, Leaf sprinted over to Linda. Then he loped back around to me. My phone cord wasn't long enough for me to place the lamp back on the end table.

Attempting to do a serious interview about the state of animal rescue in our country with a rescued cocker spaniel destroying our living room struck me as funny. I stifled a laugh.

At this point the host asked me a specific question. My heart rate increased. I found myself out of breath. I blurted out an answer, which needed more detail. My voice sounded like it came from our cockatiel Sunshine. Linda watched, unfazed by the pandemonium. She remained professional while we were on the verge of ruin.

<hr />

Leaf's reactions to being thrust into a home with people and animals who were all strangers to him caused his anxieties to multiply. But with one innocent purchase, we were able to at last see how sweet he could be when he felt safe.

We had picked up some throw-balls and chew bones for Leaf right after adopting him. A couple of weeks later, Linda bought a stuffed toy dog at the pet store. It was a replica of a long-bodied dog with little feet and made a squeaking sound when its bulbous black nose was squeezed. The middle part of the toy made a noise that sounded like a hungry tummy in need of more dog food.

After Linda presented the toy dog to Leaf, he sniffed it and then grabbed its body in his teeth, which made it squeak. From that moment on, Leaf was in love. He took his toy everywhere with him, from room to room, to his bed, on to the couch, to the kitchen, and to his potty outside.

Watching this lonely little boy hold on to what appeared to be the first toy to which he felt an attachment touched my heart. At night and during day naps, Leaf would have his foot-long stuffed toy snuggled tightly next to his body. He'd go to sleep with his legs wrapped around it. It was as if he had never had anything so wonderful that belonged only to him.

One afternoon we noticed the toy dog propped upright against the window with its nose and eyes peering outside, while Leaf napped on the couch. It was placed in the spot where he regularly sat and watched the world go by.

As I sat on the couch later that day, drinking a cup of tea, Leaf did it again. He carefully placed his toy upright, with its nose and eyes pointing toward the sidewalk. He leaned the toy against the windowpane in such a position that if it were a living creature, it could watch the neighborhood dogs walking past our house. Then Leaf jumped on the couch and immediately went to sleep.

I was amazed at how he had placed the stuffed animal in exactly the right position. It was as if Leaf had decided to make the toy dog stand guard while he snoozed. Or perhaps he had assigned it the task of keeping watch for possible visits from neighbor dogs. I wondered if Leaf was telegraphing the message, "Won't you come in to my house? I have this great toy we could play with," to the neighborhood.

Our home, as a war zone, subsided when the cats got better at handling Leaf's incessant chasing. One afternoon Linda and I witnessed a tussle between Speedy and his canine nemesis. Speedy was stretched out on the living room sofa's backrest. He looked like a true Lion King with his gray coat and whiskers.

Leaf usually liked to settle on the same high perch, but today Speedy had claimed the territory as his. Leaf decided to hunker down on the lower seat section, ignoring Speedy's turf only inches above him. Deliberately, yet relaxed, Speedy fully extended and embedded his claws into Leaf's backside. Leaf froze and made a low yelp and dared not move without the risk of being gouged. After weeks of what Speedy must have considered as "this obnoxious dog" chasing him, he was taking his revenge. "Speedy, you made your point," I said, as Leaf waited for me to save him.

Linda got up and examined Leaf's back. "I think Speedy's claws are stuck," she said.

Speedy lifted his paw, yawned, and moved himself into an even more comfortable position. Leaf quickly sped away to take his nap elsewhere.

We wondered what we should do to control the behavior of this small dog the vet had called "a troubled teenager," which is essentially what he was. And so we eventually enrolled him in a beginning class we called Training 101. With time, patience, and more knowledge about how to handle a dog like Leaf, we hoped to help him trust us, adjust to being around other people, and heal.

CHAPTER NINE

Leaf in the World

ALTHOUGH WE KNEW NOTHING OF LEAF'S PAST OTHER THAN THE SKETCHY information we received from the animal shelter, it was becoming clear that he definitely had history. I got a glimpse of the baggage he brought with him almost every day.

One afternoon Linda, Leaf, and I were on our way to the pet store. When we stopped at a red light, Leaf started growling at a large man who waited on the sidewalk street corner, just as he had done to another man after our first walk around the lake. "What is it, Leaf?" Linda asked. He quickly took on the job of being Linda's protector and barked, growled, and barked again at the fellow. When the light turned green, Leaf calmed down but repeatedly looked back to make sure we were not being followed.

We were becoming accustomed to Leaf's erratic mood shifts. Instantaneously he could switch from frightened to protective to wagging his tail enthusiastically. By the time we arrived at the store, Leaf excitedly bounced around the backseat. He loved this store where dogs were encouraged to sniff to their hearts' content.

Every Wednesday I took Leaf to doggy day care, where he had a full day of playing with smaller dogs, munching on dog treats, watching Animal Planet in the playroom, and being treated as a VIP guest at this resort for dogs. We hoped that going where staff supervised him and the other trained and untrained dogs would help him become more social. He'd get a lot of exercise and give us a break from all his issues.

In spite of his abandonment fears, Leaf loved the facility and the time he spent there. Whenever either Linda or I dropped him off, he'd bolt out of the car toward the door, eager to meet up with his playmates. At the point of departure, though, when we handed him over to one of the staff, he often piddled on the linoleum floor. We couldn't tell if this was from excitement or fear. I felt some hesitation at leaving him. When I'd call the receptionist later in the morning, she would assure me that Leaf was having a blast. Evidently after we left him, he'd adjust quickly and focus on the task at hand, which was playing to his heart's content.

One of the staff, a young Latino man, affectionately called him a Spanish name that he said meant "little leaf." Our dog had a fondness for the man and wagged his tail wildly whenever he saw him.

One day after work I arrived at the doggy day care to take Leaf home. I entered the building and peered into the large playroom, which had a glassed-in upper wall. In the middle of the room, a large man stood observing all the small dogs. I hadn't seen him there before and figured he must be a new employee. Clean-shaven, with short hair, he wore a gray button-up shirt. The man stared down at twenty dogs milling about on the floor. Leaf was nowhere in sight.

"Where is my dog?" I asked with a note of panic in my voice.

A woman staff member at the reception desk replied, "He's in the back of the room."

I was horrified to see my dog sitting inside a locked cage while all the other dogs were having fun.

My mind reeled with assumptions. Was Leaf being treated badly because he was adopted? Was he not perfectly behaved in their eyes? Thankfully, one of the employees came over and said, "Leaf was playing all day. Around 4:30 he got so focused on Rufus, we thought it best to let Leaf have some quiet time."

The employee pointed to a dog that looked like a house slipper with legs. Rufus scuttled across the floor and wove in and out and underneath dogs more than twice his size. Knowing how Leaf insanely tries to chase squirrels and rabbits, I immediately understood why they would have to give the furry little dog a rest from my genetically programmed hunter.

The large male dog-watcher opened Leaf's kennel. Our dog ran out of it fearless, happy, and full of energy. He wiggled over to the man and wagged his tail as the big guy petted him. But the second he spotted Rufus, Leaf's obsession returned and he took off after the delicate little dog, ready to continue a barrage of rough play. It was obvious why the staff had to monitor his behavior. I appreciated that Leaf hadn't held it against the male rule-enforcer. He had accepted the kennel time-out session with an attitude that seemed to say *I get it. I'm out of control here. Let me take a nap.*

Leaf, who should have been frightened of the man based on his body mass index, hadn't judged him by appearances. He overcame deeply embedded signals of danger and trusted what he felt in his heart about the person.

Linda and I discovered new things every day about what frightened Leaf. Our previous dogs had short hair, so we'd never needed to find a groomer for them. We didn't know what to expect from the experience or how groomers did their work. When Leaf needed his first grooming, we looked for a place that would give him a good cocker spaniel haircut. We took him to a groomer in an upscale area of town where many people passed by boutique shops while walking small-breed dogs whom they took everywhere. The groomer at this place, a middle-aged woman with curly brown hair, looked grim when I went to pick up Leaf. "I had to put a muzzle on him," she said.

"Why?" I asked, surprised at her comment.

"He growled at me when I tried to brush his back end."

After I brought Leaf home, sporting a cheery red bandanna around his neck, Linda and I discussed the groomer's comments. Did she have an issue with our dog because she wasn't used to working with a tough, streetwise guy like Leaf? We decided to try one more time with her and to look for a different groomer if it didn't work out.

When I brought Leaf in for his second grooming, neither of the groomers looked happy to see me. I picked him up four hours later, and the groomer said, "I love dogs and I know you adopted him from a shelter. He doesn't like to be groomed, but I'll keep working with him. Maybe he'll adjust."

I hoped that Leaf would eventually make friends with this groomer. I appreciated that she was willing to let him stay as a client but figured we needed to have an alternate to whom he might relate better.

At the dog park one day, Linda overheard a man talking about a great groomer named Patty who was always booked up months in advance. We decided to see if we could get Leaf in to see her for his next grooming. Patty, as it turned out, had over thirty years of experience. We believed she could handle Leaf. With her firm voice and love of dogs, there was no reason to doubt that Patty would know how to keep him safe as well as well groomed.

—◦—

Leaf's tendency to dominate everything and everyone in his universe caused all kinds of challenging situations. He upended my life with his problems and endless needs. Because of this, Linda nicknamed him Alpha Dog of the World. After reading more about dominant dogs, we realized that because Leaf had been neutered late in life at a year old, he had already developed all the habits of a high-testosterone male.

I felt his behavior was more complex than needing to be the guy on top, however. His small size, vulnerability, and fearfulness revved up his instincts to take care of himself. He couldn't count on anyone else to do the job. So he made sure people and animals knew not to mess with him.

At first, not knowing any better, we thought Leaf's actions were cute. While out on walks, he'd jump up and place his two paws on the shoulders of even the bigger dogs. He'd stare into their faces and make sure they knew he was the absolute leader of any pack.

"He is fearless," Linda would say. But bigger dogs were not impressed with the self-appointed neighborhood leader.

Determined to make Leaf better adjusted to people and other dogs, I took him to a small fenced-in dog park near our house. We arrived after five o'clock one evening, and about twenty dogs and people were already there. *This will be perfect,* I thought, *for helping Leaf find his social place among other dogs.*

"OK, boy, go play," I said encouragingly. I opened the gate, and Leaf ran into the park with the gusto he showed while disrupting our radio interviews. He looked back at me to see if I'd entered the park with him. Then he proceeded to run and play with the bigger dogs.

For a moment I thought we had found the place that would be his equalizer. Watching him guardedly, I felt like a nervous and protective dad. Will the other kids like him?

He stood on his hind legs and placed his paws on the shoulders of every dog he met. The big dogs ignored him. Their attitude seemed to be "whatever." Or they appeared to be mildly amused by his attempt to be alpha.

Young Leaf's swagger and attitude irritated a medium-size mixed-breed dog with white and brown markings. The dog had large, powerful jaws. Alpha Dog of the World did not intimidate or amuse "Jaws," and he snarled at Leaf through bared teeth. This escalated into a growl that lasted more than a few seconds.

"Leaf, come!" I yelled as I ran toward him. I had no doubt this dog could kill him. I grabbed Leaf with both hands and lifted him up over my head as high as I could.

Jaws lunged at Leaf repeatedly. He jumped so high that we stood face-to-face. But I was of no interest to Jaws. His wild and angry eyes focused on Leaf.

I held the little black ball of fur above my head. Jaws snarled and growled. His behavior made it clear that he'd do anything to hurt him.

The dog's person finally ran over to gain control. "You shouldn't have brought your dog here," he mumbled, as he snapped on Jaws's leash. With a furious gesture he yanked and pulled his snarling dog out of the park.

Although the perpetrator had left, I was so stunned by the dog's viciousness that I was not about to put Leaf down on the ground. I carried him in my arms to the car and examined every inch of his body. "I don't see anything, boy. Are you OK?" To my amazement Leaf looked normal. He wiggled his butt and wagged his stubby tail. I did a careful second examination. No wounds or bite marks.

Instead of a frightened, trembling victim, Leaf appeared to be the exact opposite. He was like the cowboy in an old-time Western who swaggers away from a bar brawl, eager to claim he has kicked butt.

"Leaf, you're a brave boy!" I said and gave him a bear hug. Still not quite comfortable with human touch, he froze. Here I was, his savior, and he was ready to take me on too. My big embrace had sent him over the edge. I understood. Bear hugs would take time to get used to. Hugs from strangers would too.

I silently prepared to take action whenever I saw a well-meaning person approach him with his or her arms outstretched heading straight for Leaf's adorable face. In these circumstances, he almost always issued a warning growl. I'd have to quickly intervene. People who don't ask permission to pet a strange dog or rush to get up in a dog's face don't understand that dogs interpret this movement as aggression. We soon figured out that we'd need to block people from grabbing at our dog to pet him.

I was fascinated to see Leaf's behavior evolve at the dog park, especially when Jaws wasn't there. He became fixated on a big, slow-moving, black-and-tan collie mutt named Norman who'd lie in the sun with his prized possession—an orange ball—resting between his two front paws. According to Norman's owner, the rescued dog kept his ball with him all the time at home and in the park.

One day Leaf walked over to where Norman relaxed and without hesitation took the ball and ran like a shoplifter. Norman chased after his ball for twenty minutes. Although the large old dog probably needed exercise, having this upstart steal his ball was sacrilegious. When Norman finally got it back, he no longer relaxed with it in the middle of the park. Instead, he kept it in his mouth.

A day or two later, Leaf and I returned to the dog park with his favorite, small, red-and-white ball. He never tired of having me throw this ball for him to chase. This one had all the characteristics of a perfect ball. Its smooth surface allowed for good bouncing, and it was small enough for Leaf's mouth to easily hold.

Norman suddenly lost interest in his orange ball and chased Leaf's red-and-white one, forcing Leaf to run the entire time. He had to protect his property by keeping the ball firmly gripped in his mouth. "What goes around comes around," I told Leaf as he sunk his teeth deeper into his perfect ball.

CHAPTER TEN

The Building of Life

In my dream I stand outside a gigantic domed structure. At first, it appears to be made of steel, brick, and stone. It looks solid and finite from the outside. Upon a second look, though, I see that the structure does not follow physical rules. It changes, shifts, and grows organically with no visible limits.

I watch a never-ending line of thousands of people of all ages and races move swiftly into the building. I know some of the people very well, although their names are not coming to my mind. Others, I may have seen sometime in the course of my life. But most of the people in line are strangers.

I hear a few people saying, "This is the Building of Life." Although no one tells me what is in this building, I seem to know its contents. I am aware that it contains countless rooms filled with everything imaginable. There are vast collections of art and all the books of the world. It has within itself various kinds of architecture as well as forests, lakes, and oceans. All life experiences are also represented in the massive structure. Everyone who is in line, that is, everyone with a ticket, may move from room to room after entering the building.

All of these people have tickets. My hands are empty. I do not have a ticket.

I look around to find that the ticket counters are closed. I panic. This must be a terrible mistake. I see Linda, the love of my life, standing in line with our dear friends. They are moving very quickly into the building. They are leaving me behind. Nobody turns back to acknowledge that I even exist.

Why don't I have a ticket? What have I done wrong? I am supposed to be with them. Why have I been abandoned? I try to catch up with Linda, but she is so far ahead. How will I ever be with her again?

I push my way into the line, hoping that no one will see that I do not have a ticket. Everyone notices and they glare at me with hostility. "You do not belong here," some say. Others sneer at me, "You are not one of us." I am devastated. I do not know what has happened or why.

Linda is gone. I am alone and forgotten. It is as if I never existed.

A PAT ON MY SHOULDER WOKE ME UP. LEAF HAD JUMPED UP ON MY SIDE of the bed. With shaking hands, I reached for his soft body and wrapped my arms around the little dog. I glanced over on the other side of the bed. Linda was there, still asleep.

"It was a dream. A nightmare," I whispered to Leaf and hugged him tightly into my chest. I was surprised that he let me. His soothing touch helped my racing heartbeat to slow down.

The disheveled sheets indicated that I must have been thrashing about, frantically searching for the elusive ticket counter. I listened to the steady intake and exhale of Linda's breath, but her serene face in the morning light did not comfort me. She, with everyone else I had ever known, had left me behind. Leaf lay still and drifted off to sleep on my chest. I chided myself for not being able to shake off the anger, desperation, and confusion I'd felt in the nightmare.

Later that morning I sat in the living room with Linda. We drank our coffee and glanced out the picture window at children boarding the school bus across the street. I told her about the vivid dream. With his front and back legs fully extended, Leaf lay flat on the gray carpet in front of me and listened intently.

At first I wondered if I should talk to Linda about the nightmare. I did not want to burden my wife with what to me seemed like a premonition of catastrophic loss. But did she need to be prepared? What if the dream presented something that I knew inside of me but hadn't been able to face?

Linda listened quietly while I described the dream. She asked, "Did you try to go back into the dream and finish it?" I told her that I woke up with a start. Leaf had been there to comfort me. Her face turned pale.

For a few moments we sat silently. The sounds of children's laughter on the sidewalk had ended with the arrival of the school bus. Linda got up and put her arms around me and rested her head on my shoulder.

"It's only a possibility." I cringed at the tremor in her voice. We both knew from our spiritual studies that dreams have meaning. They often warn the dreamer of things to come. "Maybe it's what could happen in some alternate universe. But not here. Not to us," she assured me. I squeezed her shoulder, unable to speak. "And besides, I'm not letting go of you."

I yearned to believe her soothing words. Like Jaws going after Leaf in the dog park, the dream wouldn't let go. Besides, I could tell Linda wasn't as certain as she tried to appear. Her assurances had sounded more like questions.

More than anything, I wanted to believe that the dream was unimportant, a perfectly understandable but inconsequential expression of anxiety. Yet I couldn't shake off the sensation that I'd foreseen the outcome of the brain aneurysm and surgery. It wasn't the happy ending I needed.

Leaf stood up and came over to us. He stared at me with his penetrating coal eyes. Then he jumped onto the couch and sat by my other side. He lowered his body next to mine and put his head on my knee. I stroked the smooth fur on his forehead. The pall of the dream draped over me like a shroud.

During the next few days, Leaf started acting oddly. He'd paw the living room coffee table until any newspaper, envelope, or magazine on top of it fell to the floor. With great focus and attention, he shredded them into tiny scraps. Each time I discovered scattered papers on the floor, I'd ask, "Leaf, what are you doing?" His behavior puzzled me. He'd never been like Taylor, who gnawed on anything that looked chewable. Why had he suddenly started ripping up papers?

As if trying to answer my question, Leaf would pick up one of the smaller shreds in his mouth and bring it to me. As soon as he delivered one piece, he'd grab another shred with his mouth and give it to me. With great determination, he persisted by tearing larger pieces of newspapers and magazines and gripping them in his jaws. He'd repeatedly shake his head and rip them into fragments. Then he'd bring the scraps to me. "Stop!" I'd finally yell at him.

I'd either scoop the papers off the floor or leave the living room so I could have some quiet and drink my coffee elsewhere. With all I had on my mind, I was not in the mood to deal with my dog's new way of acting out. I had no idea why he was making such a mess. Having to pick up after him annoyed me. Why couldn't he just behave and leave me alone?

Eventually, I was so frustrated that I gathered up magazines or newspapers from the living room coffee table and brought them to the adjacent dining room. I stacked the papers in the middle of the table where Leaf couldn't reach them. It wasn't exactly the best spot, since we had to move them aside in order to eat our meals. But at least the coveted items were no longer targets of Leaf's strange obsession. Moving the papers out of his reach finally forced him to stop the weirdness.

The more I thought about the nightmare and my exclusion from the "Building of Life," the more Leaf followed me around the house. He slept underneath my computer. He climbed onto my old lounge chair and watched me when I dressed for work. Perhaps I was imagining it, but it looked to me as if my gloom and anxiety weighed heavily on his young shoulders. He'd been through so much loss in his young life. I began to feel guilty over the possibility that I could be causing him more distress.

I wasn't able to reassure him that everything would be all right. The dream had shaken me to my core. Would my dog, still emotionally fragile, have his world rocked once again? What if, as my dream had predicted, I had been denied a ticket to the Building of Life? What would happen to Linda and me? What would happen to Leaf?

Chapter Eleven

Leaf's Strategies

With the brain surgery looming, I worked hard to hold on to my concept of normalcy. My daily routine consisted of going to work at my day job and writing at home in the evenings and on weekends. Life with my wife and our pets was especially important now. After the dream in which I lost everybody I loved and cared for, I appreciated each waking moment.

I especially enjoyed observing Leaf's slow progress from fearfulness to trust. With his startling intelligence and amazing ability to communicate and strategize, he was a perfect subject to study. I took volumes of notes on our adventures together. Surely I would write about Leaf in depth someday. My growing affection and respect for him brought us closer as friends.

Leaf was the most deliberate and careful dog I'd ever known. He pursued what he wanted but only after assessing each situation and deciding that the time was right for him to act. At our local small dog park with its picnic tables and shade trees I had the opportunity to watch him repeatedly use strategies and problem-solving skills to get what he wanted. What he wanted on one occasion was to play with the ladies, or at least one lady in particular.

About six months after we adopted him, one of our visits to the dog park turned out to be different from all the others. We were there for about fifteen minutes, while Leaf played with several large dogs. From

the corner of my eye, I saw a dignified woman wearing a long, pale-pink overcoat. She walked a bulldog who wore a shocking-pink collar that glinted in the sunlight. I would not have expected a woman in such an impeccable outfit to bring her pooch to a lowly dog park.

Nonetheless, both the woman and her dog arrived at the gate. The woman looked down and asked, "Ethel, do you want to play here or go for a nice, peaceful walk?" Ethel immediately pulled away from the gate. She wanted the walk. With great dignity, the woman and Ethel began their slow stroll down the sidewalk next to the fence.

Leaf studied their interaction. When Ethel led the woman away, he clearly wanted to do something to change the bulldog's mind. Running like a bullet to the fence, he kept pace with the retreating Ethel. He wiggled, waggled, squealed, and barked. In doggy language he tried to convince her to come into the park. He spotted a tennis ball, picked it up in his mouth, ran back to the fence, and dropped it in front of his paws to tempt her. Leaf was determined to persuade Ethel that playing with him would be preferable to taking a boring walk.

My boy finally got Ethel's attention. She glanced over at him and slowed down. Leaf gave his last squealing appeal. He wiggled his whole backside and then quietly sat. How could Ethel resist a romp with a fellow who looked so cute and playful?

There was a moment of silence. Ethel and the woman looked at Leaf. To seal the deal, Leaf splayed out his front and back paws and furiously wagged his tail.

That did it. Ethel made a U-turn so fast that the woman lost her grip on the pink leash. Leaf sprang to his feet and hurried to greet Ethel with unbridled enthusiasm.

Once inside the dog park, the woman unhooked the bulldog from her leash. Leaf immediately covered Ethel with multiple doggy kisses. With unrestrained joy, he sniffed her all over. His expectations of how much fun the bulldog would be were fulfilled. Ethel at first played hard to get—this is a game Leaf dearly loves. Then she dropped the elusive female charade, and the two of them ran side by side with abandon. They kept pace like two slow race horses sprinting around a track. Their fur touched. Leaf's ears flopped in the wind. In a *Lady and the Tramp* moment, Ethel forgot her good breeding and let herself have fun with a scruffy former shelter dog.

The woman asked, "Is that your dog?"

"Yes, his name is Leaf. He's our little teenage boy."

"Ethel normally prefers walking," the woman murmured.

Ethel and Leaf circled back to where we stood. The other patrons of the dog park watched the drama with Leaf and Ethel unfold.

"He loves it here," I said. Leaf picked up a stick in his mouth and took it back to Ethel.

"He has certainly captured Ethel's heart." The lady looked confused as she placed her white-gloved hands in the pockets of her pink overcoat. "Ethel doesn't normally like other dogs."

Suddenly, Ethel snapped at Leaf's nose. Leaf adroitly backed away a couple of inches. He had become a master at avoiding scratches and bites from our cat's training sessions. Rather than finding his new girlfriend's rebuff unnerving, Leaf looked at Ethel with even more adoration. *She likes rough play,* his face seemed to say.

He grabbed a stick and tempted her to get it from him by laying it down at his feet, inches away from Ethel. *Go on. Snatch it.* She made a slight move toward the stick. Leaf grabbed it back in his mouth.

Ethel, unaccustomed to not getting whatever she wanted, turned her head away as if to say, "Enough of him. Let's go." Leaf dropped the stick. He backed away so Ethel would have a better chance to take it. But Ethel was already trotting toward the gate. The woman hooked the leash to Ethel's pink collar. She reached for the gate latch.

Leaf ran to the gate. Ethel glanced at him, still obviously enjoying his attention. As the woman fiddled with the gate latch, Leaf gently grabbed the pink leash with his mouth and pulled it out of the woman's hand. Then he led Ethel back into the dog park with the leash gripped in his mouth.

At first the woman appeared flustered. "Oh, no, no, we have to go," she called. "Ethel, come back. Ethel!" She walked to the two dogs and picked up Ethel's leash, holding it more firmly this time. Leaf, having made his final argument, let it go.

Leaf sat and watched Ethel and the woman return to the gate. The woman turned around and said, "Leaf, next time we see you in the park and Ethel wants to play, we'll be back."

Ethel appeared to grin at the promise of more fun to come. Leaf, of course, took it all in stride. After all, what lady can resist a charming tramp?

CHAPTER TWELVE

Just When You Think
It Can't Get Any Worse

THE NIGHT BEFORE THE ARTERIOGRAM DR. NUSSBAUM HAD ORDERED, I had another vivid dream. In the dream I experienced massive lightning strikes and flashes of pain across my mind's eye. I felt synapses become disconnected; some were rerouted. In the nightmare my brain became less functional than it was before. I felt the pain of what was about to happen.

The dream could have been more directly related to the arteriogram ahead, but it also reflected the arc of my experience. I rested for a few minutes, then got up. I heard the phone ring and wondered who was calling so early in the morning.

"Hello," I said as I picked it up.

"Hi, Allen. This is Bob."

Bob Lawton has been a close friend of mine for many years, even though we live in different states and don't call each other often. He's always been a generous, kind person. His spiritually oriented view of life gave him the emotional toughness he needed to be successful as a firefighter. Bob spent his career saving lives and dealing with perilous situations. He served on the front lines, often putting himself in danger to help others.

"Bob, what a surprise," I said, now totally awake.

"I had to call you. I know what you are going through now." Bob got quiet for a moment and then continued. "I had a dream with you last night. I saw it."

Leaf sat nearby and didn't take his eyes off me. I assumed he wanted breakfast. "Your call couldn't come at a better time."

"The light flashes and pain; we were together. I feel bad for you."

"That you know what's happening to me means a lot. You made my day."

With that, we said our goodbyes. I prepared to visit the hospital.

Later that day I experienced in the operating room exactly what I had felt in the dream just a few hours earlier. All the pain, flashes of light, disorientation, and exhaustion came as if on cue. The dream had prepared me for the real situation. And because of Bob's call, I felt that a friend had understood.

But all was not well. A few days after the arteriogram, a painful swollen spot appeared where the arteriogram needle had entered the artery in my groin area. I called Dr. Nussbaum's nurse Jody and told her about the problem. She set up an appointment right away for me to have a sonogram of the area that had swelled to a large, hard bump.

The sonogram went well until the technician's expression changed from relaxed to tense. She needed to send the test results to the doctor for review. About an hour later, when Linda and I asked the receptionist if we could leave, she said that someone would come out to talk with me.

We were oblivious to the commotion my sonogram had caused. While I telephoned my office to pick up messages and check on projects, the radiology doctors summoned Nurse Jody for a consult. After we'd been in the waiting room for an hour, Nurse Jody and another nurse arrived to talk with us. They both looked serious.

The sonogram nurse said, "It was good you found the knot in your leg and got it tested this morning." She added, "We're in a precarious situation right now." A few seconds passed while I thought grumpily, *What else? I have meetings scheduled.*

Nurse Jody was hesitant as she spoke. "You have a blood clot near the knot you found," she said, "and it's in a bad location." The blood clot had nothing to do with the large bump, she explained, but it had helped them discover it. "We can't give you blood-thinning medication because of the scheduled surgery. Even a small bleed could be deadly." The two nurses explained that I must have an emergency procedure before my major brain surgery.

Within the short span of about six weeks, I had gone from being a healthy man in the prime of his life to one who faced two life-threatening conditions. Later I learned that the deep vein thrombosis caused by the clot, like the brain aneurysm, typically displayed no symptoms. This is why both conditions were so deadly.

In the case of the aneurysm, unrelated dizziness (and my wife's insistence) had driven me to the doctor. Now, a painful swelling, not caused by the blood clot, had prompted me to call Dr. Nussbaum and schedule the sonogram. Both the dizziness and the swelling disappeared after accomplishing their task of moving me in the right direction. Here again, with my life pitched over a cliff, I was being held above the precipice by what I could only ascribe to divine intervention.

I quietly listened to Nurse Jody and the sonogram nurse while I struggled to take in what they were telling me. The sonogram nurse took Linda's hand in hers. "You and Allen should not leave the hospital," she said. "The doctor is recommending an emergency procedure. We'll insert an IVC filter device in your primary vein to protect your main organs. The clot could travel through the major blood vessel that returns blood from the lower body to your heart. This is surgery, and you may have to stay in the hospital overnight after the procedure."

I called our dear friends of many years, Arlene and Aubrey Forbes, to ask them to take care of Leaf while I had the emergency procedure. Arlene, a nurse by profession, is slender and tall and an accomplished singer and dancer. Aubrey is one of my closest male friends. He was a member of a small writers' group Linda and I started that met Thursday evenings. Although his management job kept him moving in a fast-paced world, he brought kindness and gentle nobility to all of his actions and words.

We had previously entrusted Arlene and Aubrey Forbes with our house key, and they were familiar with our pets. In addition to being the logical choice to ask for help, Linda needed to confide in Arlene (they called each other "Sis") about my new medical situation.

At this point my insecure dog still wasn't friendly with anyone who came to our house, invited guest or not. He'd hurl his body against the front door with such vehemence that grown men stumbled backward down the porch steps to get away from him. Somehow, he made himself appear large in spite of his small size.

For his safety and our peace of mind, we kept him inside the large dog crate (his cave) whenever we were away for short periods of time. We were still not confident he could, or would, hold his potty break needs until we returned home. The crate kept him from using our carpet like grass. Staying in the crate also decreased his need to howl with fear at people who walked by our house or tree branches that rubbed against the roof on windy days. The crate and its comfortable dog bed helped Leaf feel more secure.

I didn't know how Leaf would respond to Arlene and Aubrey entering our home when we weren't there. They would have to release him from his crate, put a leash on him, take him outside, and feed him. We'd never rehearsed that routine. I tried to communicate with Leaf by visualizing his face and thinking, *Be nice.*

The last thing I needed right now was for my emotionally distraught dog to have a setback. I did not want Arlene and Aubrey to become wary of him. *Please, no growling while I'm in the hospital,* I mentally telegraphed Leaf. *Be nice.*

Arlene and Aubrey drove over to our home after work. They walked in with their unique ability to put anyone, animal or person, at ease. When they let Leaf out of his crate, he wagged his tail and licked their hands. While they shut the crate door behind him, he eagerly gobbled down the dog food they placed inside. They called us at the hospital with the reassurance that Leaf had been "a perfect gentleman." I was grateful to our friends for helping and to Leaf for cooperating. I guess he had gotten my message to be nice.

As I went through the accelerated admittance process for emergency surgery, I quickly filled out the paperwork for a health directive and the "Five Wishes" forms. It stipulated that the hospital wouldn't unnecessarily prolong my life if I was only being kept alive mechanically. It seemed reasonable to not keep a body alive without real life within it.

The doctor, who would insert the umbrella-shaped IVC metal filter that was designed to stop blood clots from entering major organs, stopped by the cubicle where Linda and I waited. Nurses prepped me for surgery. The surgeon looked young to me but did not have Dr. Nussbaum's exceptionally youthful appearance. He implied that anything involving blood clots is risky. I would be sedated and feel discomfort but not severe pain.

After the surgeon left, an attendant wheeled me to the surgery room. I remained fully conscious. As my gurney passed through hospital hallways and under the fluorescent lights, scenes from my past came pounding back to regain my attention. One in particular was from my days as a cop in Atlanta.

~~

One late afternoon when I was still a rookie cop, I patrolled a residential neighborhood. The bright sun shone in a cloudless sky, making it hard for me to see beyond the glare. A woman ran into the street and yelled for me to stop the police car. She pointed toward the end of the block. "A man has been stabbed!" she screamed.

I immediately informed dispatch and asked for backup and an EMS unit. I ran over to the man, who lay face-up on the sidewalk. The knife that had pierced his heart lay in the road a few feet away. His girlfriend, reeling with grief and shock, stood over his body. She cried and begged for someone to help him. Other people from the neighborhood gathered at the scene.

I spoke into my hand radio and asked dispatch for the EMS unit's estimated time of arrival. I knelt down beside the conscious man, who looked to be in his early thirties. As a new cop, I immediately knew that I wasn't prepared to handle such a situation. Still, I was the one on the scene, and I had to do my best.

I tried to stop the bleeding by placing pressure on the wound with my hand. The man looked up at me. While I stared back into his eyes, I realized he was aware that death was near. I continued to apply pressure. He reached for my right hand as if to tell me to stop.

People around watched, horrified. I centered myself and tried to remain calm. I placed my hand on his shoulder. The light and awareness inside his eyes slowly darkened and went out. His sobbing girlfriend collapsed into the arms of an older woman nearby.

The EMS unit arrived and took over attending the victim. I spoke into my radio and gave a lookout description for the suspect. Other officers found the perpetrator several blocks away. He turned out to be a recently released mental patient who had been visiting his mother. He'd found a knife in his mother's kitchen, grabbed it, ran out the front door, and attacked the first person he saw.

The victim, nibbling on a bag of french fries, had gotten off the bus with his girlfriend. One moment a french fry was in his hand, the next he was looking into a cop's eyes, knowing his life was over. Death came just that quickly and with just that much apparent randomness.

Once I had been delivered to the operating room, the anesthesiologist administered conscious sedation. The surgeon inserted the tube into the main artery at the back of my neck. Because I was still conscious, I watched the X-ray screen display the tube. The procedure went without a hitch, and several hours later I was released from the hospital. Linda and I drove home, with both of us deep in our own thoughts. I reflected on the bizarre twists of the day.

While I rested on the couch that evening with Leaf's body sprawled across my lap, I felt thankful that once again I'd been given another chance. But then the unease crept in as I remembered that I still had no ticket to the "Building of Life."

CHAPTER THIRTEEN

Facing Fears

IF EVER I NEEDED A BREAK, IT WAS NOW. THE BEST BREAKS, WHICH TOOK me away from all my worries, were with Leaf. Our newest discovery was the massive Minnehaha Off-Leash Recreation Area, otherwise known as "dog-park heaven." Dogs romped on the beach and swam in the river. They chased sticks.

Walking through the eight-acre dog park, with its wooded trails and the Mississippi River running through it, Leaf indulged his passion for leaves. He had two or three favorite spots where he threw himself onto the ground and rolled in dirt and leaves with gleeful abandon on every visit. This always brought smiles and laughs from me and the other dog-park patrons.

Leaf was showing me much about survival, growth, and love. I carefully observed everything he did. He and his doggy viewpoint fascinated me. He had proven to be a calm yet determined fighter, using his intelligence, skills, and intuition to focus on his goals. He was a survivor with a curious twinkle in his eyes. At this park Leaf loved to run, play, and explore. With an enthusiasm that matched my dog's, I became part of his world on our great adventures together. No worries here.

One day I watched Leaf face one of his greatest fears: losing control of his favorite ball. While this was not exactly in the same realm as brain surgery and blood clots, it was crucial for a dog who had few coping skills around loss.

I threw his ball into the river, making sure it didn't float out too far. Leaf dove in after it with only a bit of hesitation. He evaluated the distance and possible challenges of a swift current. With the ball floating only a few feet from shore, he repeatedly retrieved it for me to throw again.

We walked a long distance to an undisturbed inlet with dark, still, deep water feeding it from the fast-moving river. Passing boats made small waves. People chatted with each other while sipping coffee they'd brought to the park. A few ducks swam nearby. The water's shadowy surface hid whatever unknowns lurked below.

When I threw Leaf's ball into the mysterious water, he hesitated. He looked at the ball and at me. I said, "You can do this." The ball had floated only four or five feet from where he stood. The water rose up to his knees on his short legs. He could easily walk or swim and retrieve the ball. But venturing out into the deeper water would take a leap of faith. Who in their right mind would jump into murky, still water, not knowing what hidden dangers lurked there? I saw in him that day my own fears of what lay ahead for me.

A young man in jeans and a plaid shirt sat on a log nearby and watched Leaf. His large mixed-breed dog was also a rescue. Like Leaf, the dog had become a wonderful friend and companion. The man called out words of encouragement for Leaf to go and get his ball.

Leaf barked at the ball as it slowly floated on the placid black water. He whined and whimpered as if pleading for it to return on its own. The ball wouldn't cooperate. Leaf took one careful step after another into the water. Three or four feet to the left of where Leaf's ball floated, a tree branch had fallen into the inlet. Leaf looked at the branch. He assessed the situation and worked out a strategy.

Carefully, he jumped up onto the dead limb. He slowly walked toward his ball. As he drew closer, I could tell he felt conflicted. Should he continue on his quest or retreat to the safety of land? Bravely he forged onward. After arriving at the spot, Leaf had to make another decision. Would he jump into the ominous water or retreat from taking a dive into the unknown?

By then the man's dog sat beside him. They both observed Leaf's dilemma. The man noticed Leaf apply his problem-solving skills by using the log as his bridge. He said, "That's the most endearing thing I've ever seen a dog do." I found it amusing and touching for a stranger to become so involved in Leaf's challenge that he rooted for him. "That's one smart dog," he added. "You can tell he's afraid. But he worked out a unique way to get back his ball."

I said nothing to Leaf. He needed the freedom to make his own decision.

He held tightly to the branch with his paws, then jumped into the murky water. His head and body dipped under the surface for a second. He emerged from the dive, spotted his ball, grabbed it in his mouth with determination, and swam back to shore.

A bright light of new confidence emanated from Leaf. The other man and I were enthusiastic about Leaf and his victory. He had faced the unknown. "Good boy," I kept saying. "You did it!"

As we continued our walk through the park, I intermittently threw the ball for Leaf and thought about how my recent health traumas had tested the still waters of my life. Watching Leaf refuse to give up was a lesson for how creative and persistent I'd need to be in order to get my life back. It was refreshing to see Leaf conquer fear and anxiety. He glowed with self-confidence. He had swum into the unknown. Did I have as much courage as my little dog?

Leaf demonstrated another survival skill I'd need in my own journey. Because of Leaf's prior abandonment and my experiences with police work, we both had to revive our trust in people. For Leaf, this test of courage took the form of allowing himself to show affection to a species that had cruelly betrayed him.

Linda had always wanted a dog who would let her pet and cuddle him. Leaf would have none of that. Linda could pet him, and he'd allow it. But if she leaned down to kiss his head, he offered nothing in return. One day she confided, "Oh, how I long for one more of Taylor's sweet doggy kisses."

We don't remember the exact date when it happened, but a few months after Leaf became a member of our family, Linda bent down to kiss him on his forehead. He raised his head and examined her face carefully, as he had on our first visit to the animal shelter. Then with his raspy pink tongue, he planted a big, wet kiss not on her mouth, but on her nose.

One kiss. She said, "I think I'm going to die of happiness."

From that point on, their kissing sessions burgeoned from one to two to three to four carefully placed nose licks. Within another couple of months, Linda was the thrilled recipient of kisses in the morning, kisses in the evening, and definitely kisses at suppertime.

Around the time that my medical drama shook our lives, Leaf started a new bedtime ritual. He'd jump up on the bed, paw at my side, pull down the covers, and prepare it for his favorite playmate's arrival. Then he'd roll over on his back while I rubbed his tummy.

After Linda was tucked in with her head propped up on pillows and a book in her hands, Leaf would sit at her shoulder and gaze lovingly and intensely into her eyes. Then carefully and methodically, up and down and sideways, he'd lick her nose for as much as a minute.

Satisfied that he'd settled her in for the night, he'd say goodnight to me with a lick or two. Linda got many more kisses, I guess because Leaf knew she needed them. All the pain and anxiety she felt over the possibility of losing her husband to death or permanent disability drained out of her as she and Leaf held their nightly love fest. She liked to joke, "I have a husband and a fella."

After he completed the kissing, Leaf would rest his head on Linda's shoulder and fall asleep while she read. He'd stay there until she turned off the light. At that point he'd jump off the bed and go back to sleep on his adjacent dog bed or in the bedroom doorway—ever protective, ever watchful. Linda and I would fall asleep listening to his gentle sighs, snores, and snorts.

One night as she closed her book and prepared to go to sleep, Linda turned to me and said, "I've been kissed by many dogs in my life. No kisses have been sweeter than Leaf's. Maybe it's because I had to earn them."

Leaf had taken the steps toward committing to his relationship with Linda and me. With his new nighttime ritual, he expressed gratitude and love. And that's what you do with the ones you love—you kiss them on the nose.

Chapter Fourteen

The Manual

About a week before my scheduled brain surgery, night after night, never leaving his post, Leaf stretched out flat on the floor of my office, while I worked on what I called "The Manual." It would contain all the financial and other details that Linda would require if I died or was incapacitated from the brain surgery. I had decided that creating "The Manual" was something I wanted to do alone. I told Linda that I could move faster by myself. Really, though, I didn't want to put her through all the emotions such a document would dredge up if we sat side by side to create it. And besides, what if she had an emotional reaction to "The Manual" the way she had to "The Memo"?

Early on in our marriage, we had agreed to share household tasks. While I'd handled the day-to-day financial duties, we'd discuss any big decisions or purchases. After we began writing together, our division of labor also included my being in charge of creating and maintaining websites related to our Angel Animals Network. I maintained access to many Internet sites and functions that required passwords. "The Manual" would help Linda take over my duties and keep our household running while I recovered.

Our arrangement had worked well over the years, especially since my day job required much travel. My wife and coauthor could focus solely on the complex and time-consuming procedures involved with our books' story contributors. She could handle most of the requests from editors and marketing people who needed input from us, even when I was temporarily out of touch.

Since I went to my office during the day, creating "The Manual" became a nighttime and sometimes into-the-early-hours-of-the-morning task. It took days of concentrated effort. Somehow, it fit that since I faced the prospect of not being able to live the life I wanted anymore, I was working on it as the sun set, and night overtook my world.

Looking over old bank statements, I recognized names of restaurants where Linda and I had eaten. I picked through records of bookstore purchases that had filled our shelves with writing and animal books. Movie theater stubs had mixed in with other receipts and reminded me of breaks we had taken to view new films. Would I ever hold my wife's hand at a Cineplex once again? Or munch on an extra-large, shared, buttered popcorn? I longed to call up to Linda, who was working in her office upstairs, "Do you remember when we went to Three Fishes restaurant for our anniversary last year?"

After Linda went to bed, it was only Leaf and me facing my mortality. On the upside, though, the process of creating "The Manual" was reminding me that I needed to do everything possible to win the battle and continue my life's journey.

I shuffled stacks of important papers, made phone calls to verify information, and visited websites for screen grabs and jpegs. I created flowcharts to make instructions for complicated processes that would allow a smooth transition of our duties. As I attempted to depersonalize "The Manual" and keep my emotions in check, I designed it the same way I had written software manuals for work with elements such as "click this" buttons, overviews of each section, step-by-step instructions, task assignments, and testing. *I can do this,* I kept reminding myself. But making business manuals didn't require forcing down a lump in my throat.

Occasionally Leaf would raise his head and focus on me with his prescient eyes. For an instant, I would feel a glimmer of hope that Linda would only need to temporarily refer to "The Manual." He'd plop his head back down between his two front paws and let out a loud sigh. Were my emotions taking a toll on him? He'd lost some of his vigor since I'd started working on "The Manual" and looked exhausted. I felt guilty at the thought that he might be taking on my burdens.

When it came time to gather all the necessary documents for filing medical and dental bills and possibly having to apply for disability, it overwhelmed me to think about the cost of each procedure, test, and visit to the hospital. They were adding up to beyond what our less-than-stellar insurance covered. How would we deal with the new round of medical bills? We still had to finish paying for four major surgeries that had vanquished Linda's breast cancer. I'd come close to losing her then. Now she was facing the same prospect with me.

Unlike the memo fiasco, I did not go through a ritual or ceremony when the time came to present "The Manual" to Linda. I simply walked upstairs to her office. Leaf padded along behind me. I told her that it was finished and where she could find it on my bookshelf. I hoped that no more discussion was needed. It had already been painful enough to design it.

Later that night, though, I found Linda in our white-walled bedroom, sitting on the edge of our bed. She clutched a handful of tissues and dabbed at her eyes. I walked in and sat next to her. Holding her hand, I reassured her that "The Manual" would only be necessary during my recovery period after surgery. "But what if you don't make it through this?" she asked.

She had finally spoken the unspeakable. Her words sent me reeling. Constant problem-solver that I am . . . this time, however, I had no answer. "I'll get rid of the thing," I said and bolted off the bed. I felt a sudden urge to destroy the document I'd worked so hard to create. Its very existence showed a lack of faith that I would survive.

She pulled me back to her and continued to cry softly. "I'll read it while you're at work tomorrow." Then she wrapped her arms around my chest and grasped me tightly. Her body shook as she sobbed into my shoulder. Through all the doctors' appointments, hospital tests, procedures, and preparations for my surgery, she had stayed strong. She was a professional woman who had previously run her own business and managed entire corporate departments. She didn't cry often, which is why it unnerved me so much when she did.

"You know I am going to make it," I said. I silently cursed my voice for not having more conviction.

"I know. I know." But in her eyes I caught a glimpse of the last thing I wanted to see there—a sliver of doubt.

Now that "The Manual" was completed, I could sit in my old tan recliner and relax. But the thoughts that swarmed like moths around a flame allowed for no rest.

One afternoon before my surgery, I took Leaf to the dog park near our home. This was the same place where he had fallen in puppy love with Ethel the bulldog. The small dog park had become my refuge. Leaf was fast becoming my BBF—Best Buddy Forever.

Life pounded me from all directions. Emotionally beaten and mentally exhausted, I pondered the age-old questions about what is truly important in a person's life. Was I supposed to leave a legacy of the work I had done and the people I had affected? Without that legacy, why had I lived at all? The blood clot and brain aneurysm had brought me to the realization that in a moment, my time on earth could be over. Why did I have such a strong desire to survive? Was my purpose not yet identified or fulfilled?

With his example, Leaf was teaching me to live in the moment. His funny antics, curiosity about all things, and genuine love of life refreshed my viewpoint. His appreciation for the smallest acts of kindness reminded me to stop thinking about my problems and what I didn't have and cherish

all I had taken for granted. It was as if he was saying, "You're missing out on the fun and joy around you."

On this particular day I sorely needed to be reminded of this. Leaf and I entered the dog-park gate, which was next to an old, and what I had thought was deserted, railroad track. A residential area, a grade school, and swing sets and slides for smaller kids were visible from the park. It seemed an ideal place for getting away from the daily grind.

While I had been writing "The Manual," Leaf had been subdued and tended to stay nearby as if keeping an eye on me. I was glad to see him eagerly enter the park and bolt through the gate after I opened it. Normally he waited with anticipation for the windup and throw of his ball. But now he looked up at me and then sprinted toward the back part of the park, which was closest to the railroad track. Still unable to shake off my negative thoughts, I followed him.

When I caught up to him, I saw the engine and first cars of a long freight train approaching. Leaf jumped up on top of a picnic table, sat very still, and thoughtfully watched the engine. It rumbled along and Leaf trembled with excitement, just like a little boy.

Ignoring the other people and dogs in the park, Leaf kept his eyes glued to the train. The depth of his interest surprised me. But Leaf had always been a different kind of dog in that way. He noticed everything. Like an investigator observing details and gathering facts, he seemed to evaluate each event and store the impression of it in his memory bank. I could tell that something was going on in his intelligent brain that day. He never lost focus on the long train.

While he sat on top of the picnic table, I slid onto the bench next to him. He did not move even slightly. Our heads were at the same level. Both of us watched, fascinated, as the freight train moved by slowly. We had front-row seats and a perfect view from a safe distance. We could see the differences in the colors and models of each. We could hear the clatter, banging, and squealing of the wheels. We were two guys, on a warm spring afternoon, sitting together and watching a train go by.

Then, without warning, the horrid mental pounding of my life's greatest regrets began plaguing me again. I wondered if, like my friend and mentor Bruce, I was coming to the end of my watch.

Leaf glanced at me for an instant and then immediately turned his head back to the train. I got the feeling that rather than fearing it, he was impressed with the enormity of this moving mass of metal. While watching Leaf's admiration for something much bigger than himself, I thought of how small I felt. Larger-than-life events barreled through my mind like this massive train.

I looked at Leaf and the freight train again. An idea came to mind: Let me give my problems to the freight cars. Each car would take one of my painful memories and concerns about the future and noisily but efficiently move them away from me. Was this a brilliant or silly idea? I figured that anything that eased my anguish at this point was worth a try.

Was this what Leaf wanted me to do? As soon as I had the thought, he broke his concentration on the train, glanced at me over his shoulder, and licked my cheek with his soft tongue. OK, BBF, I will do it.

I felt lighter with each passing freight car. I unloaded one worry after another and watched the train's cars take them away. My chest relaxed and I breathed deeper. It's amazing what the mind can do, and even more amazing was what a canine friend can do.

I looked over at my dog and felt so much love and gratitude for him. Completely immersed in the present moment, he continued to watch the massive train slowly go by, carrying my heavy load with it.

Part Three

Uncertain Outcomes

*I talk to him when I'm lonesome—like I'm sure that he understands
When he looks at me so attentively and gently licks my hands;
Then he runs his nose on my tailored clothes, but I never say
nought thereat,
For the good Lord knows I can buy more clothes, but never a
friend like that!*

—W. Dayton Wedgefarth

Chapter Fifteen

Rallying Allies

MUCH HEAVINESS LIFTED AFTER THE TRAIN EPISODE. I COULD THINK more clearly now. Increased clarity led me to accept the fact that I needed more help than Linda or Leaf could provide. I'd need additional allies—people who would assist me in the battle for my life.

Being a private person, I'd always found it difficult to ask for help. Besides, I didn't want to be obligated to anyone. And I've been the one who solved problems and gave assistance when asked. I repeatedly told Linda that nobody should know about my personal medical situation. She talked me into telling a few friends, so she could have support too during the process.

Arlene and Aubrey were two friends we relied on. They had taken care of Leaf the day I stayed at the hospital for the IVC filter procedure. In preparation for my brain surgery, their friendship also helped me come to a better state of mind. Because Arlene was a nurse, her approach to what I was about to experience had the practicality that would jolt me into becoming more proactive.

"Allen," she told me over the phone one night, "you need to visit the hospital floor where you'll be recovering after surgery." Her voice conveyed the experience and authority she must have mastered during twenty years of nursing and managing a ward of nursing staff. "Introduce yourself and Linda to the staff. Let them know your surgery date. Find out what the hospital's infection rate is. What percentage of nurses are independent contractors, not regular hospital staff? How long will you be in ICU? I have two pages of questions for you to ask. I'll e-mail them."

The conversation with Arlene made me feel empowered. Her generosity gave me an enthusiasm I hadn't felt since the fateful call from Dr. Lucas. From her real-life experience, Arlene made me realize that visiting the hospital and introducing myself to the neurosurgery ward's head nurse and staff would show that I was invested in my care.

When I received her e-mail, I saw that it included many more important items, such as:

- Make sure to have adequate pain management. It helps the healing process when pain is under control.

- Find out what kind of name badges are worn by hospital staff members.

- Have advocates throughout the experience who stay with you. Let them know where to take breaks. Let them get familiar with the hospital layout.

- Be sure licensed nursing staff are actually doing the daily care, and no one else gives shots.

- Find out what medications you'll be taking and their side effects.

- In addition to getting to know the head nurse in charge of the unit and the nursing supervisor or director, ask to meet the floor nursing staff.

Most of all, she emphasized that Linda and I shouldn't be shy about asking direct-care staff to wash their hands before touching me. With Arlene's special brand of humor, she added, "You don't need no stinking infections!"

I knew that Linda and I could be watchful, to the best of our abilities. We'd bring bottles of hand sanitizer and place them in strategic locations around my hospital room. But the main line of defense would be to encourage hospital staff to view me as someone they cared about rather than a faceless, nameless patient.

My new plan was to talk to the head nurse in an effort to emotionally engage her in my survival and full recovery. So many people come in and out of recovery wards. I knew from my father's many hospital stays what slipshod places they can be. I wanted to make myself stand out in a good way.

I also borrowed a page from Leaf's playbook. He had placed his favorite toy in our home's picture window with the intention of attracting a friendly doggy playmate. I'd use our Angel Animals books to befriend the head nurse and staff of the neurosurgery ward. Armed with my typed-up sheet of questions and stash of books, Linda and I made an unannounced visit to the head nurse's office a week before my surgery.

"Hi, my name is Allen. I'm going to be a patient here next week," I said softly to the nurse who typed at the nurse's station computer. Why did I suddenly sound like someone who was tentative? What happened to Proactive Allen? Hospitals can be such intimidating, formidable places, I reasoned. And I'd be coming to this one without the certainty of leaving it alive. No wonder I'd lost some steam.

With an easy sweet smile, the head nurse, Amy (not her real name), held out her hand, and I shook it. "Very nice to meet you," she said.

The conversation we had with Amy was similar to friends chatting at a social gathering. This busy head nurse didn't rush us. Instead, she seemed pleased that a patient would make the time to have a tour of her ward. She liked that we wanted to be introduced to people who would be taking care of me. I guess this type of previsit was a novelty.

Amy was delightful and oriented toward giving quality service. She loved our gift of books. We signed each one for her and the staff. Even though we had sprung the visit on her, she was attentive with careful answers to our prepared questions. I shook hands and chatted with the ward nurses, orderlies, residents, and other medical staff assigned to the neurosurgery recovery unit.

That day I became an individual to them with a full life ahead of me. I'm not saying they don't view everyone in this manner. They're professionals

who take great pride in their work. But for me, the visit gave me my power back in a positive way. Until then, I had felt mostly powerless. Arlene hit a home run with her suggestion. Leaf was also an inspiration.

The fact that everyone we met at the hospital had an animal story to tell didn't surprise me. This kind of thing happens to us all the time. It was fun listening to escapades and experiences the staff had with their pet dogs, cats, birds, horses, and other animals.

One of the last things I needed to take care of before my surgery was to make a list of my unfinished business. Of course, Leaf was at the top, with his name in all capital letters. I had promised him a forever home with both Linda and me. That commitment alone would keep me going. Other items on my list included taking a long, oceanfront vacation; having more fun, laughter, and play time with my wife and our family; and moving to a more spacious home. I even wrote "take dance lessons"—a real stretch for an uncoordinated guy like me.

As I thought of everything I wanted to achieve, I let myself dare to hope that someday I would at least attempt all of it. But in the back of my mind, I couldn't help but wonder what lay beneath the murky waters of my future.

Chapter Sixteen

"Be Nice, Leaf . . ."

During the final days before surgery, Leaf rarely left my side. He would touch my leg with his nose, bring his ball for me to throw, and distract me from my thoughts. My normally standoffish boy actually wanted me to spend more time petting him. That was a treat for me.

His insistence finally won out. "OK, boy, let's go," I said as I pulled myself away from my desk one afternoon. Soon we were driving to the small nearby dog park to get some fresh air and exercise. I glanced over at Leaf quietly watching the world outside the car window. For a moment, he looked angelic, innocent, and sweet. Was I catching a glimpse of the companionable dog he would become after he healed from his previous traumas?

I hoped this wasn't merely wishful thinking. Earlier that day, while I walked him around the neighborhood, he had barked and shot a little growl at a nice lady when she tried to pet him. She yanked her hand back, gave Leaf a wide berth, and quickly walked away.

I looked at Leaf and asked, "So why didn't you like that lady this morning? She only wanted to pet you." He looked at me as I lectured him—a parent reasoning with a child who requires firm guidance. "You need to be nice and considerate. I want people to like you. Don't you want to be liked?"

Since we'd adopted him, I came to realize that Leaf was nothing like most other dogs. Most dogs I'd known wagged their tails and wanted to be friends with people. I always assumed it was natural for dogs to love people and people to love dogs. Leaf proved pickier than other canines. He definitely did not buy into the worldview that all humans were his friends. He appeared to think the reverse. How could he trust people? They hadn't been trustworthy.

Leaf let out a big yawn while I continued my lecture. Frustrated, I tried to get him to understand how important it was to me for him to treat people, even ones he didn't know, with respect. "Let's make a deal!" I said, sounding like the host of a television game show. "When you see someone you don't know, do anything nice you can think of."

Leaf looked out the window, appearing oblivious to my chatter. *Yeah, sure. Whatever. Now can we get to the part where you throw the ball for me, and I run and catch it?*

When we arrived at the dog park, Leaf entered with his usual gusto. My king of the park, head held high, walking tall, surveying all his dog and human subjects.

I pulled his rubber bouncy ball out of my pocket and threw it. Lately he had been even more interested than usual in running after the ball. People at the park commented that Leaf had more retriever instincts in him than some of the retriever breeds that came there. It was fun for all of us to watch him run with enthusiasm on his short legs, his large ears flopping, as he pursued the ball. Sometimes I'd make it bounce several times. He seemed especially pleased when he caught it midbounce, before the ball rolled flat along the ground.

I noticed an older gentleman in a short-sleeved shirt who was throwing a yellow tennis ball for his small, white, fluffy dog. Sometimes the dog would chase and retrieve it but more often, he'd ignore the ball. This meant the man had to get off his bench, hobble over to the ball, pick it up, and throw again. The man looked tired. He finally sat down to rest. The tennis ball lay on the ground a distance away and neither he nor his dog seemed interested in getting it.

Leaf observed the interaction between the man and his dog. As soon as he dropped his ball at my feet, he tore after the yellow tennis ball. He grabbed it in his mouth and slowly walked over to the man on the bench. Casually he dropped the ball at the man's feet. Then he patiently waited for the man's gnarled fingers to gently pat his head. The man looked up at me and said, "Your dog is nice."

Leaf purposefully glanced over his shoulder and straight into my eyes as if to say, "See?"

Assured I had gotten the message that he could be nice when he wanted to, Leaf trotted with his head high toward me. In that moment I felt like anything was possible—even lecturing to a dog and actually having him listen. Was our little dog discovering the blessings of being an angel pup?

Just as I thought we were finishing up our time at the dog park that day, he took another opportunity to let me witness his true character.

Normally, Leaf runs to the gate when it's time to leave. He carries his ball in his mouth and looks like he's ready to go home and enjoy his nap. That day, though, he stood about twenty feet from the gate near the only other dog left at the park. A woman sat on a bench watching the dog. Up to that point Leaf had ignored the dog and woman.

He looked at me and at the lone dog and then back at me again. I held the gate open. Why didn't he run over to it? I felt a nudge, my inner voice, telling me to ignore the heat and my longing for an air-conditioned car.

Leaf and I walked over to the woman, who gently talked to the dog she had named Murphy. "I rescued him only twenty-four hours ago," she explained. She went on to say which shelter Murphy had come from.

"That's the same place we found Leaf," I said. Both dogs had been abandoned there and left to fend for themselves.

Murphy looked traumatized, scared, and alone even with the woman's constant reassurance. "I'm your forever mommy," she told him repeatedly.

"How is Murphy doing?" I asked.

"Since the time I adopted him, he's been so upset that he hasn't gone to the bathroom." The note of worry in her voice made me empathize with her immediately. I recalled all of the conversations and concerns Linda and I had about Leaf's initial elimination issues.

As we talked, I threw Leaf's orange ball for him a couple of times. Murphy watched Leaf running after it. His expression conveyed that he wanted to join in the fun. I bent down, focused my eyes on his face, and said, "Murphy, you look very handsome."

Murphy touched his nose to my hand. I slowly rolled Leaf's orange ball down the hill again. This time Murphy ran after it. He stopped after about five or six feet and hurried back to his mommy. The lady was delighted and praised him.

Leaf observed the scene and wagged his tail with increasing momentum. He came up to Murphy, and the two dogs stood nose-to-nose for a few seconds. Their tails wagged in unison. Leaf didn't make any gestures to play. Perhaps he sensed that any sudden movements might scare the timid dog even more. But I was pleased to see that they had made a dog-to-dog connection.

I talked more about Leaf's past with Murphy's new mommy. She commented on my dog's healthy and strong personality. "He's strutting like he's fearless," she said. I knew it had to be encouraging for her to see that an abandoned shelter dog could eventually regain self-confidence.

"Murphy has a bright future," she said. "He will be spoiled, loved, and safe in his new home." I told her about the great doggy day care in the neighborhood that had helped Leaf become more socialized. The tension began to fade from her face.

Now a more relaxed Murphy walked a few feet away to a grassy area. Leaf had used it earlier for his potty break. Murphy sniffed, circled the area, sniffed again, and at last was at ease enough to eliminate.

My dog and I walked to the gate once more. Leaf carried his orange ball in his mouth. He constantly surprised me with his intuitive abilities. Leaf had listened to his inner voice about Murphy and had responded with all the love in his heart.

I did not know it at the time, but what I had witnessed—Leaf's ability to empathize and be there when someone needed him—would become my lifeline in the days and weeks to come.

Chapter Seventeen

The Ticket

The day before surgery my mother, sister Gale, and Susan, our adult daughter, were flying from Atlanta to the Twin Cities for my "surgical procedure." I assumed Mom had told everyone that this was my preferred phrase for brain surgery.

I felt grateful that Mom, Gale, and Susan had each left Georgia and their jobs to be here on such short notice. They'd incurred travel expenses and would spend their time sitting in a hospital waiting room rather than sightseeing Minneapolis and St. Paul. Our son, Mun, wasn't able to get off work to come, but he kept in touch with us by phone. My mother, who disliked flying, was determined to be with me during and after surgery. My brother, Richard, helped Mom and my sister with making their travel arrangements.

Although I had a lot on my plate during the weeks leading up to my surgery, I still managed to fill it up with worries over my family's visit. I felt like I should plan activities for them. Linda found it amusing that my main concern was whether or not they would have a good time. "They're not coming to be entertained," she reminded me. "They want to be here for you." I was deeply touched. Their presence would make me feel loved.

All my concerns immediately disappeared the moment they came off the plane. Susan's warm smile spread across her face when she saw me. The sight of her immediately lifted my spirits. I was reminded of what she used to tell me when she was a teenager and I expressed anxiety about something: "Chill, Dad." Mom looked worried but also pleased with herself for making the flight. Gale's face was etched with sweetness. The three of them chattered away as if they were going to a party.

When we asked them where they wanted to eat, Mom said without hesitation, "Red Lobster."

At the restaurant Mom barely glanced at her menu. She knew exactly what she wanted. The rest of us needed a little time to choose our meals. Normally at family gatherings, my sister Gale has always been the one to say just the right thing at exactly the right time and to help us see the humor in almost any situation. Today, I could tell she was nervous. She turned to me and said quite seriously, "Are you enjoying your last meal?"

Everyone at the table got quiet. I didn't know how to respond. What did she mean by my "last meal"? We all looked at each other and burst into laughter, drowning out Gale's explanation that she meant my last real meal before hospital food. The resulting belly laugh helped release much of the stress I still held on to.

While we finished our meal and waited for the check to arrive, Gale blurted out what the rest of my family members were probably thinking. "How will I know you're all there after the surgery?" she asked.

Without hesitation I answered, "I'll say, 'Red Lobster.'"

—◦—

So many things have the word "last" preceding them when a person is about to have brain surgery or any operation in which any number of things could go wrong. I either had to deal with the emotions that welled up in me as I prepared for the worst or stuff them back down.

Taking care of details in the weeks before had forced me to live moment to moment, even as my mind wandered to places of fear and doubt. Linda and I practiced driving the route from the hotel to the

hospital. We'd sleep there the night before the surgery, and she and my family would stay through the week following surgery. But in spite of all my efforts to focus on the present, the nightmare I called the "Building-of-Life dream" and my desperation for a ticket to it haunted my thoughts.

Each morning during that last week, I sat in my recliner chair with Leaf in my lap and his head propped up on a plump pillow. I talked to him softly about what was to come. I told him how many nights I would be gone. "You'll be happy playing at doggy day care and have plenty of food," I explained. The doggy day care, where Leaf got his exercise once or twice a week during his first winter with us, also had a boarding facility. It relieved my anxiety to know he'd be in a place where he felt safe and knew the staff. I'd hold the sides of his finely contoured face with its turned-up nose and look deeply into his eyes. "I need you to help me when I come home. I want lots of your healing kisses." Leaf would gaze up at me with his wise ebony eyes, sigh, and then fall asleep to the sound of my voice.

Once we had dropped Leaf off at the day care and had settled into the hotel, I called to check on him. The staff reported that he was asleep in his kennel on the soft dog bed I'd brought to be boarded with him. I'd included an unwashed T-shirt of mine with his baggage. The staff person told me that Leaf's nose rested on top of the shirt. I knew he was breathing in my familiar scent.

Linda and I spent the night holding each other tightly and hoping this wouldn't be the last time. Linda is the love of my life. We're soul mates and need each other for life to be of any value. I wouldn't be me without her. Would we ever be the same?

As I lay there, I remembered Dr. Nussbaum's crisp color chart showing an aneurysm that had a well-defined neck for easy clipping. I wished mine was more like the one displayed on his office wall. Neither of us could sleep. I was anxious, thinking about the surgery, Linda, and how frightened Leaf might be when he woke up alone. Would he wonder if I'd be returning soon to bring him home? Would I be returning?

Early on the day of the surgery, Linda and I drove from the hotel to the hospital. The blazing sunrise mixed with a deep blue sky made it a beautiful morning, yet we both were somber. To lighten our dark mood, I said, "So, another *normal* day in the life of Allen and Linda Anderson." Leaf liked it when I said, "Everything is *normal*." To him normal meant no big changes. Normal was his cue to relax.

I glanced over at Linda. She turned her head and studied my face. Usually she'd smile when I said Leaf's favorite word. But today she had no smile for me. Instead, she gave a deep sigh and focused on the road ahead. After all our years of marriage, I could tell that she didn't have the energy or inclination to lighten what was about to happen.

After I parked the car in the hospital lot, neither of us made a move to get out. Instead, we sat silently. Linda squeezed my hand. "I love you," she said.

"I love you too."

At that moment, I felt so much appreciation for how supportive she had been throughout this ordeal. She had taken care of so many details—double-checking test results, saying whatever encouraging words I needed to hear, and making sure the pets were cared for when we had appointments to keep. Even with all the extra strain, she had kept up with our work and deadlines.

She looked out the car window as if something vital drew her attention. I sensed that she was trying not to let me see the fear in her eyes. She knew my nature too, and that I'd keep trying to find a way to fix things. But surgery day had arrived, and I had no more fixes. We got out of the car, held hands, and walked toward the hospital doors.

A smiling woman in her midthirties with short blond hair like Linda's met us and noticed that we looked lost. She introduced herself as the chaplain. She escorted us to the elevator and gave us directions.

"Odd that the first person we see today is the chaplain," I said to Linda. She nodded in agreement. My disturbing thoughts made me spiral down the rabbit hole: *Chaplains are needed to be with the grieving family after a terrible loss.*

We found our way to the admitting room. With a business-like composure, I filled out the necessary forms. The clerk was a middle-age woman with short, curly gray hair and sympathetic eyes. She looked over my answers. I just wanted the paperwork to be over before I gave in to my urge to grab Linda's arm and head for the door.

After check-in we walked to the surgery-prep area. Linda listened with an intense and serious look on her face while the nurses told us details of what would take place before and after surgery. By this time an emotional paralysis had replaced my anxiety. I had slipped into "this can't really be happening" mode. Surely a doctor wouldn't soon be cracking open my skull and performing surgery on my delicate brain. What was I doing here? Why were these women I don't even know talking to me so much?

Dr. Nussbaum and Nurse Jody, and then the anesthesiologist, visited us in the surgery-prep area to tell me what was to happen that morning and ask questions like, Are you allergic to any medications? Have you ever had a negative reaction to anesthesia?

Did I answer their questions? I must have. They left and didn't come back.

As if just a witness to the scene, I watched myself sitting in the small examination room. I felt uncomfortable in the new itchy, short-sleeved shirt I'd purchased to wear to the hospital. I reassured myself that I could still call the whole thing off, maybe even return the new shirt. My skittering mind settled on thoughts of Leaf. A slight smile lifted the corners of my lips. I remembered how he always made the most out of whatever life handed him.

"Linda," I asked, "If we get through this, we can't keep doing things the same way."

"We won't," she assured me.

In the prior weeks, Linda and I had talked a lot about changes and improvements we would make to our lives. As we walked with Leaf trotting between us around the lake one day, she'd rattled off lists of things I needed to live for, to fight for—a long and happy life together, seeing our children have grandchildren, writing a blockbuster book. We promised each other that after this nightmare was over, we'd stop working so much. We'd take time off and just be. Laugh more. Love more.

Even after charting an exciting, new, after-surgery course, I wondered if we would revert to Leaf's favorite state of normal. For us, that meant multitasking like crazy and rushing to meet impossible deadlines. Right now, even that harried lifestyle sounded good to me. After all, it beat the alternative.

While we waited together, I returned to the reality of the situation and my surroundings. I looked around the tiny cubicle and saw the bustling hospital staff going about their duties beyond the partially drawn curtain. My hands gripped the vinyl arms of the beige-colored chair where I sat with my feet propped up. I listened to the murmur of other presurgery patients talking softly to their loved ones in adjacent cubbyholes.

A young nurse with an African accent came into my cubicle, glanced down at my hand, and said, "No metal is allowed in surgery." I looked at my wife's stoic face and caught a glimpse of her pain. An ache rose up inside me when I slipped the gold band off my finger and handed it to her. She carefully placed it in the front compartment of her purse. We held hands once more. She kissed my cheek.

At the request of the nurse, Linda left to go to the waiting room across the hallway where my family and friends had gathered. I had never known it was possible to feel this alone in spite of all the people milling about a busy hospital pre-op floor.

I changed into a white hospital shirt and robe. Another nurse came in and assisted me with putting white thrombosis stockings on my legs and green slippers on my feet. She left for a few minutes to care for other patients. When she returned she said, "You have a few minutes before surgery. Do you want to spend time with your family?"

The nurse explained that I had too many visitors for her to bring them all to the pre-op area. I said yes to her suggestion of going to the waiting room, forgetting how silly I looked in my new hospital ensemble. I wanted to see familiar faces, to talk with anyone who knew me and could confirm that I still existed.

I also kept thinking of Leaf and catching fleeting glimpses of him in my mind's eye. He looked at me with his characteristic crooked smile. Someone had once called it Leaf's "Elvis lip."

The nurse guided me through the hallway to the waiting room. I spotted Linda right away and felt immensely relieved. She looked calm now, almost warrior-like in her determination that I would survive this. Seeing her made me feel whole again.

Seeing the rest of my family all together felt like I was attending a party in my honor. The scene was the closest thing to a wake that anyone could have while still being alive. Gale, Susan, and my mother were there. Our friends Arlene and Aubrey rounded out my "A-Team."

Everyone looked tense, worried, and unsure of what to say to a man who might not even remember them by the afternoon. Should they acknowledge that this might be the last time they would ever see me? They remained silent, waiting for me to speak.

I hugged each of them and sat next to Linda. Glancing over to a large fish tank in the middle of the room, I was startled when an image of Leaf's face reflected off the glass.

I hadn't been given any medication yet that might have caused me to have visions. Still, I saw my sweet pup gazing at me lovingly. I blinked my eyes and looked again. He was gone. But in this brief vision, I saw him frantically grabbing slips of paper off the living room table and holding them in his mouth. The action was identical to what he'd done at home after I'd had the Building of Life dream.

The night before, while Linda and I lay together in bed, she'd said, "Tomorrow, they will let you talk to all of us before you go into surgery. You don't need to be the life of the party, crack jokes, and try to make us feel better. Just be real." Linda knew me well, and her advice was good. I sincerely thanked each person for all he or she had done to help.

Gale, looking fragile and scared, sat next to my mother. I told her how grateful I felt that she'd made so many sacrifices to be with me right now.

Susan gently attempted to pump me up with her positive attitude. I'd asked her earlier to keep her younger brother informed about my progress throughout the day. My mother forced a smile, but her eyes couldn't conceal her worry. I assured her of my love and gratitude.

With his easygoing outlook on life and hearty laugh, my good friend Aubrey was as solid as granite. And I knew Arlene, the compassionate nurse, would look after Linda. But in spite of my attempt to focus on these loving people, I continued to worry about being separated from all of them forever as my dream had foretold. When the nurse signaled that it was time for me to return to the pre-op area. I kissed Linda once more and drew upon whatever courage I could muster.

Once in pre-op the nurses placed warm blankets over me, and the anesthetists, wearing blue scrubs, injected a tube in the vein in my arm. A man with a gray beard and glasses started an IV in my other arm and casually asked what I did for a living. I said that my wife and I wrote books about the human-animal bond.

Like so many others, the man launched into telling his own Angel Animals story. He said that when his son was a teenager, the boy had brought a dog home from an animal shelter but was not able to take care of the pup. Before long the rescued dog became the father's. He admitted to being glad it had turned out that way. The canine companion had shown him nothing but devotion over the years and had actually brought his son and him closer because they both loved the dog.

The two men preparing me for surgery stepped back suddenly. A blond woman in her midthirties appeared where their faces had been. Calm emitted from her. I remembered her as the hospital's chaplain. She reintroduced herself to me.

"Is it OK if I say a prayer?" she asked.

"Yes, thank you."

Her prayer was filled with phrases like "trust in God," "cycles of life," "all is in the divine plan," and "relax in God's love." Flashes of blue light sparkled around her head. Seeing the blue light reminded me that there is an essence of life that crosses the thin line separating the physical world from the heavens. For me, this essence can be seen as light at moments of heightened awareness.

The chaplain gently held my hand for a moment and quietly left the area. After she was gone the thought flickered through my mind that her visit and seeing the blue light around her would be a great send-off to the heavenly worlds. I relaxed with comfort in my belief that regardless of how things worked out, soul, the part of me that does not die, would live on.

An attendant wheeled my gurney into the surgical suite. Strong arms lifted me from it onto the surgical table. I'd soon be unconscious. In the corner of the room I saw bright flashes of blue and white light. A divine and loving presence was with me. I had nothing to fear. I surrendered to whatever was meant for me.

The breathing mask hovered ten inches above my face. It slowly lowered. I heard the bearded man on the surgical team say, "You are safe. We will be with you through it all."

Before the mask reached my mouth and nose, I again had a vision of Leaf's face. He still carried a sliver of paper in his mouth, as I had seen him do at home and in the reflection in the waiting room fish-tank glass. In that split second my sweet cocker spaniel dropped the piece of paper he had gripped so tightly in his mouth.

In my inner vision I reached for the paper Leaf had dropped. When I touched it I suddenly knew without a doubt what it was, and a calm understanding flooded my consciousness. Leaf had brought me my ticket. He'd been trying to deliver it to me all this time. Along with family and friends, I would awaken and enter the Building of Life.

Chapter Eighteen

The Surgical Procedure

LINDA LATER TOLD ME THAT WHILE I WAS IN SURGERY, AT A TIME WHEN my life engaged in a dangerous dance with mortality, a memory surfaced in her mind. Every spring large black crows perched in the tall oak and pine trees in our backyard. Their loud caws to one another were unnerving. Ever since we interfered with their natural cycle the previous spring, their caws had become louder whenever we walked from our house to the garage.

It happened on a walk with our yellow Lab, Taylor. We found a baby rabbit who had escaped the crows when they raided a bunny hutch. One of the birds probably dropped the bunny from his claws. The baby lay in the grass, eyes closed, but still alive.

With Taylor watching curiously, I scooped up the small rabbit in my hands and immediately became aware that the atmosphere bristled with fury. "You stole that crow's lunch," Linda said. She pointed to a crow about the size of a hawk. He screeched at me from a nearby tree branch. His buddies gathered with him and joined in a rage-filled chorus.

We brought the baby rabbit inside and made him a nest in a cardboard box. Then we placed the box with some water and chopped-up vegetables and fruit in a secure area under our deck. We hoped that the fencing around the bottom of the deck would keep him safe, until he was strong enough to return to his hutch or his mother found him. We replenished the nest and water for the baby frequently. After a couple of days, the box was empty. We never saw the bunny again.

A year later, after rescuing the baby rabbit from the crows, we now had a twenty-five-pound cocker spaniel hanging out in our backyard. He made sure nothing there would harm him on the ground level. Unfortunately, he wasn't in the habit of searching for predators in the sky.

One morning Linda let Leaf out in the backyard to take care of his bodily needs. She went back into the house but suddenly had an inner nudge to check on him. From our back deck she watched Leaf sniff the dew-coated green grass. Then she noticed a huge crow hovering on a high branch of our old oak tree. He glared down from his perch, ready to nose-dive on to the back of our unwary little dog. The crow focused silently on Leaf as if he were thinking, *There's breakfast!*

Linda immediately called to Leaf to come back in the house. Our little guy remained oblivious to the fact that he might have been a tempting target. Could this have been the same bird whose bunny I had stolen a year ago? Was the look he gave Linda conveying, *You took something I wanted. Now I'll get something of yours?*

Part of the responsibility of being a pet parent is to teach our young ones how to protect themselves. We sat down to have a talk with Leaf about the facts of life in a neighborhood filled with crows. "Leaf, every time you go outside, stand on the deck and look up into the sky," Linda instructed him. "Make sure no crows are in the trees before you run out into the backyard."

Odd as this may seem, Leaf became even more aware of his surroundings. Before venturing into the backyard, he always stood at the top of the steps on the deck and surveyed the sky and tree branches. After he was certain no crows were around, he enjoyed his outing. I had been pleased to see that our pup, even early on, was a quick study in the ways of a natural world.

As I was lying vulnerable on the operating table, Linda didn't know what would happen next. She also didn't know that Leaf had delivered my ticket.

Fortunately, Arlene joined her at the hospital chapel, where they sat together in quiet contemplation underneath shafts of gentle sunlight. Linda felt an overwhelming sense of peace. She sensed the surgery had begun.

When she returned to the waiting room, Linda heard Nurse Jody being paged, "Come to surgery. Stat." Knowing that Jody was Dr. Nussbaum's main nursing assistant, and I was his only surgery patient at that time, she felt a wave of panic pass through her body as she watched Nurse Jody rush down the hall, past the waiting room, to the surgery suite.

By now, surgery had stretched from the two hours Dr. Nussbaum had expected it would last to four hours. He had sent no information about what was happening or why it was taking longer. The delay created fertile ground for my family and friends to imagine trouble. People were already calling Linda's cell phone, thinking the surgery would be over by now. In a tremulous voice she'd had to report, "No word yet."

My wife and everyone who loved me endured the torturous wait. Naturally they wondered if there had been complications. Or worse, that maybe I'd had a stroke on the operating table.

Nearly five hours later Linda sat in another part of the waiting room, talking to her mother on the phone. She glanced over at my mother and sister. Worry clouded their faces. Our daughter Susan paced the room, trying to stay calm, and said positive things every time anyone speculated about why the hours were ticking away. Because Linda didn't want to increase everyone's anxiety, she only told Arlene that she'd seen Nurse Jody rush to the surgery suite.

Finally, with the surgery over, Dr. Nussbaum and Nurse Jody entered the visitors' waiting room. Linda quickly ended the phone conversation with her mother and hurried over to them. Dr. Nussbaum told Linda and my family that the surgery had started late. It had lasted longer due to its difficulty. The aneurysm was extremely tricky to clip, because my vessels were very thin. The shape of the aneurysm was ill defined, which we knew from the X-ray.

Each time Dr. Nussbaum clipped the aneurysm, the clip would slip down onto the main artery. He couldn't leave it in that position, or the clip would impair blood flow to the brain. "I had to try three different ways of clipping it before I found one that would last," he said. He had called for Nurse Jody to help him finish up the operation.

When we had first seen Dr. Nussbaum, he'd explained that some people don't choose to have an aneurysm clipped right away. They wait to see if it gets bigger. Now the doctor reassured my wife that I'd made the right decision to proceed with the surgery. The aneurysm's shape and location indicated that at some point it would probably have burst. Then he said something Linda will always remember. "Allen will never have to think about this again." She felt immensely grateful. Linda believed that no surgeon other than Dr. Nussbaum, with his experience and skills, could have accomplished what he did for me.

But the next twenty-four hours in the intensive care unit would be some of the most precarious hours of my life.

Chapter Nineteen

Using My Ticket

The hospital's twenty-four-hour ICU is not the kind of place a person who has just had brain surgery can easily remember. For me, this was probably because I felt as if my head had been slammed into concrete.

The hospital lights were unbearable. The gurney's wheels clattered deafeningly. People's voices struck me like bullets.

"Don't scratch," someone commanded, as I reached up to scratch my ear.

"He just pulled out a couple of stitches," someone else said.

Then I heard Linda's voice and tried to focus in on her blurry face. "You made it. You made it. You made it," she kept repeating.

There was something important I was supposed to remember, but I couldn't keep my eyes open. Assured by Linda's voice, I sank back into unconsciousness. She would be my link to whatever came next.

I have no idea how much time passed. It could have been seconds or hours.

Linda remained in the room when Gale arrived for her visit. Her blurry figure triggered a memory. "Red Lobster," I slurred.

Linda and Gale laughed. I didn't understand why. I was only fulfilling the agreement I had made to her at the restaurant. My brain still worked. I was still here.

For a split second, I saw Leaf's face.

I faded in and out of consciousness. Nurses had Linda and my family and friends return to yet another waiting room. After a shift change the ICU doors were locked. Linda got someone's attention, and a nurse led her back to my room again.

After Linda left the ICU waiting room, a woman who was also waiting for a surgery patient asked Arlene, "Is she famous?" The woman had recognized Linda from a photo in the *Minneapolis Star Tribune* months ago. It accompanied an article about the animal-rescue book we'd written. The photo showed my wife on a raised platform. She stood nose-to-nose with a giraffe from the Audubon Zoo in New Orleans who had survived Hurricane Katrina. It struck me later as one more surreal occurrence in my brain-surgery saga.

Linda said one moment that especially touched her was when Aubrey held my hand in his and said, "Glad to see you, my friend." I vaguely remember Aubrey's face. I felt his loving presence. He stood close by on my left side. The lilting Jamaican accent in his kind voice came from a distance.

A numb yet constant pain filled my head. Nursing staff regularly monitored my pain medications. Throughout the night they changed fluids bags and checked my heartbeat, blood-sugar level, and important vital signs. Their presence made me feel safe. The room was quiet. The curtains were drawn. I rested.

The next few days after ICU were a blur. My pain ranged from mild soreness to throbbing excruciation. I became a 110 percent supporter of pain-management medications.

I fluctuated from feeling I could do anything to barely being able to open my eyes. In the neurology recovery ward, the curtains stayed drawn to keep my room dark. Light hurt my eyes like a dagger stabbing the inside of my skull.

One side of my face was swollen from the surgery. My skull felt hollow. A scar stretched from the top of my head to just above my ear. A strange echo reverberated whenever I spoke. I didn't feel like myself anymore.

My mother, sister, and daughter took turns with Linda and stayed with me throughout the entire week. Because I seemed to be making a better-than-expected recovery, they all felt comfortable returning to Georgia the day before I was to go home from the hospital.

After Gale, Susan, and Mom left for the airport, Linda took a lunch break. While she was gone I called Leaf's doggy day care. I must have sounded like a drunk phoning from a bar. I don't recall much of what I said, and my speech was slurred. The person who answered assured me that Leaf was fine. I immediately went back to sleep. Leaf was doing well—that's all that mattered.

Steroids to ease the swelling on my brain agitated me. They created illusions of power and control. The nurses and Linda told me to press the call button when I needed to get out of bed. The steroids, however, made me feel like Superman. I thought I could handle a short walk to the hospital room's bathroom, but when I pulled myself out of bed, I staggered and fell full force on the hard tiled floor.

Linda returned from the cafeteria to find a nurse helping me back to bed. "He got up by himself," she told my wife. Her tone sounded a bit like snitching.

Linda was horrified. "Why did you do that?" she asked me. "Did he hurt anything?" she asked the nurse.

"No. I'm fine. Nothing wrong with me."

The nurse rolled her eyes at me as she helped to hoist my legs onto the bed. "Use your call button next time," she said.

I couldn't find the words to explain to Linda why I'd done such an imprudent thing. Desperate to be independent, I needed to prove how quickly I'd recover. Nothing had changed. I'd still be employed, independent, dependable. A fully functioning man.

Prior to leaving the office, I'd told my employer that I'd be back at work the third week after surgery. The company needed me to fly to an important client site the fourth week. "There are various suggested days for recovery, but a couple of weeks should work for a healthy man like me," I'd told the company's president and my boss. They were sympathetic and weren't trying to pressure me. But after all the time required for pre-surgery tests and procedures, I had very few vacation or sick days left.

Panic drove me to not think clearly even before the surgery. While no one told me I'd lose my job if I didn't get back to work fast enough or couldn't operate at full capacity, people who can't do the work they were hired for are sometimes let go. I clung to the belief that I could push myself to handle the job. My employee health insurance would be essential to at least partially pay the catastrophic medical expenses, and I didn't want to lose that.

To Linda's dismay, the president, my boss, and his second in command from my company came to the hospital during the first week and only a few days after my surgery to check on me. They mentioned they were in the city on a site visit and decided to stop by. They arrived at midday when I was awake and alert. This gave them the impression that I was making a remarkable recovery. I felt relieved that they saw me at my best. After asking general questions about the surgery, the men talked about the work ahead of me and wanted to know when I thought I'd be returning.

At first I thought it was nice of them to visit. Linda felt that this was a fact-finding mission. She believed they wanted to assess whether their employee would be able to work and travel. I didn't agree with her totally. They were honest, decent individuals who did a lot professionally and personally to support their office staff.

Linda cautioned the men that the doctors said I must not talk for long. She hoped they'd take the hint and not try to pressure me. She knew I was the main liaison with the major client I was scheduled to visit in four weeks.

By the time the men left, Linda was upset, and my anxiety level had soared. Their visit reminded me that my days and nights would be hard after I was released from the hospital. I knew then that the three weeks I had for healing would be inadequate before returning to work. Would I be able to pull off convincing everyone that I was back to normal? Even so, I was determined to make it happen.

Losing my job and not being normal again were in my thoughts. The president and vice president were compassionate and ready to do whatever I needed for a full recovery. But everyone was feeling tense. Our company had just been acquired by a larger firm, and there were rumors of breakups and layoffs.

Amy, the head nurse, stopped in to check on her resident pet-book author. She chatted about her pets and told us how much she enjoyed reading the books we'd given her and the nursing staff. Up to that point we were happy to tell her that my nursing care had been excellent.

Before we left the hospital that day, I felt something gnaw at me. I would have to rely on, even trust, others for my well-being. That frustrated me. I had always been the one who took care of things.

I resolved to send clear messages to everyone and myself that my brain function was not diminished. In my confused state of mind, I thought people were treating me like an invalid whenever they offered to help. Reduced to my father's dependence after his stroke, I was every bit as ready to lash out as he had been. Unlike my father, who had lived the rest of his life in miserable helplessness, I resolved to be invincible.

But just how long and to what extent would I stay out of control of my own body, of my own life?

Chapter Twenty

Leaf the Healer

After Linda brought me home from the hospital and settled me into bed, she headed out to the drugstore to pick up my postsurgery prescriptions and then to doggy day care to bring home Leaf. Meanwhile, happy to be home, I fell into a deep sleep.

Eventually my ticket-to-life deliverer bounded into the bedroom to greet me. When he smelled all the strange hospital odors that still clung to my body, he became extraordinarily quiet, attentive, and affectionate. Pulling himself up with his paws on the side of the bed, he scrutinized and sniffed me carefully. Although my prescription-drug-laced breath and swollen face must have surprised him, he still licked my cheek. There's nothing quite like unconditional love.

"Hi boy," I said softly. "How are you doing?" I petted his head and swiftly fell back to sleep.

My wife had a lot on her shoulders. She had to administer to me on a strict schedule from a portable plastic file cabinet full of pills. One day, she gave me something at noon that I was supposed to take at dinnertime. Anxious that I'd suffer some traumatic effect, Linda called Nurse Jody to confess. The stalwart and seasoned neurosurgery professional assured my wife that I'd be all right.

It was essential to my recovery that I slept in a darkened room. Linda shut the blinds and hung sheets over the curtains to allow in the least amount of light. She kept me as comfortable as possible. I alternated between sleeping, asking if it was time yet, please, for pain medication, and believing I ruled the world.

In between taking care of and monitoring me, Linda also handled all our pets' needs. Then she would head upstairs to her office to work on our writing projects, answer e-mails, and talk to friends and family about how I was doing.

To her horror, I climbed the stairs to her office one day. "I thought you were asleep!" she gasped in alarm.

"Let's take Leaf to the dog park," I said. At that moment I felt this was a reasonable request.

"How about if we go out in a day or two? After you've had time to get more rest? You've been through a lot, you know."

"Well, if you don't want to drive us, I'll take him to the dog park myself."

Linda got up from her desk. She rushed over to where I teetered on the top step.

"Come on downstairs," Linda cajoled. "I'll make you some tea."

Sounding like Homer Simpson, I crooned, "Uhmm. Tea."

She escorted me downstairs and deposited me on the living room couch. Leaf, being a good caregiver-team member, came over to seal the deal. He planted himself with his body across my leg so I wouldn't get up. While Linda made tea in the kitchen, I thought I also heard the sound of rattling metal. Was she hiding the car keys?

As the days of my recovery at home continued, Leaf worked hard to get me to become more active. He frequently brought his favorite ball to me, and his eyes pleaded for playtime. "OK, here it goes," I would say, throwing the ball down the hallway for him to chase. It wasn't our beloved dog park. But it was the best I could do.

The first day Linda drove Leaf and me to the dog park in an attempt to get back to our normal routine, I was every bit as much of a sight as the recovering patients I'd seen in Dr. Nussbaum's office. A tan baseball cap

covered the neatly stitched surgery scar that wound from the center of my skull to below my ear. It would eventually be covered by my hair. But in this early stage, its swollen pink stitches were visible. The right side of my face blossomed with black-and-blue bruises. I looked like an extra from the movie *Fight Club*.

I sat on the picnic bench, debilitated and morose. I didn't have enough strength to throw the ball for my eager dog. Instead, Leaf had to settle for Linda. He looked disappointed when she didn't throw his ball as far. Each time he brought it back, he dropped it at my feet instead of hers. His face read, *She throws like a girl*.

The day after I got home, our neighbor, a kind man with a quintessential Minnesotan accent, knocked at our back door. Linda was upstairs working, so I answered. When I saw who it was, I remembered that he had offered to cut our grass.

"I finished the lawn," he said after I opened the door. I motioned for him to come in, but he stayed at the doorstep. Maybe because this was his first glimpse of my bruised face and swollen eye.

"Thanks so much," I said. I would have liked to be more cheerful. But as he stood in the doorway, bright sunlight shone behind him and hit my eyes like bricks. My head started pounding with pain.

Trying to be helpful, he said, "You have to remember to pick up those pinecones. They got stuck in my mower when I ran over them. Almost broke the blades."

I knew my neighbor, retired from a full-time job he'd held for thirty years, meant well. He wanted me to know that I had to take care of this pinecone business if I didn't want damage to my own lawn mower.

After he left and I closed the door, I went back to bed feeling depleted that I hadn't been able to keep up with my lawn. I resolved to free myself from this uncomfortable state of dependency.

A couple of weeks into my recovery, Linda and I walked with Leaf by my side along the Mississippi River in dog-park heaven. I threw the ball for Leaf to chase, but it landed in water too deep for his comfort zone.

A small fish jumped near where his ball had landed. Leaf was not about to swim where there might be creatures underneath trying to nibble at his paws. He stared at the ball, turned his head to look at me, and barked.

Surprisingly, my little guy mirrored the determination I now had. He was not going to ask anyone for help. *I'm going to man up,* he seemed to say.

Leaf tentatively moved toward the ball, which now floated even farther away. He quickly lost his nerve and backed off. He barked at the ball again. He whined and pleaded for it to change course and return to him.

Leaf knew how to swim. He just didn't seem to be confident in himself in these rapidly moving waters. The swift river currents would give anyone pause. They might be strong enough to sweep up a small dog and carry him away.

Leaf's frustration grew. I prepared to remove my shoes and wade out to rescue my fellow's ball. Linda said, "He has so many other balls. Just let that one go."

Of course, her logic made sense. But my brain still wasn't consistently sending or receiving logical thought. "He's really upset. He needs his ball," I replied.

Before I could finish untying my shoelaces, a family walked by with its own short-legged dog trotting alongside. Their dog, a terrier-mix, took note of the situation and instantly figured out what was happening. From the shore, the dog looked at Leaf alternately pining for and glaring at his ball floating away on top of the dark water.

Without hesitation, she jumped into the water, swam, grabbed the ball in her mouth, and brought it back to shore. Her family watched the scene unfold. When she dropped the ball at Leaf's feet, they shouted, "Good girl!"

Leaf grabbed the precious ball and wagged his tail with gusto. "Thank you," I said to the dog's cheering section. They looked quizzically at my tan baseball hat and visible scar. Their expressions conveyed both sympathy and the instant revulsion I was becoming accustomed to.

"What's your dog's name?" Linda asked.

This broke the Frankenstein monster spell. "Lizzy," they answered. They proceeded to tell us what a great dog their little pooch was.

"She's very brave," I added, as they turned away to continue their walk. "Thank you," I called after them. I felt grateful that I hadn't needed to get my feet wet.

After they left, Linda looked relieved. "I'm so glad that little hero kept you from going in after Leaf's ball. What if you had slipped on the rocks?"

As we resumed our walk, I thought about Lizzy. She'd made the conscious decision to help a dog she didn't know. No complaints. No fuss. Just do the good, kind deed, the right action, and be on your way.

Maybe receiving help from others didn't have to be such a sticky proposition after all.

I had to go back to my job in just a few days. I was not about to take disability. I assumed that the stigma of having been incapacitated enough to qualify for disability would follow me to any new job. Anxiety over what might happen when I went on my next business trip filled me with stress. I'd have to do computer-software training for a class of strong-willed, talkative people in my weakened and often confused state.

I would need all the help I could get. And I'd better learn how to ask for and accept it.

Chapter Twenty-One

Alpha Leaf

My brain had been tampered with, and its matrix of connections disrupted. My frontal lobe, the section of the brain that regulates emotions, had slipped from what I hoped was tip-top performing condition into obvious unreliability.

Supposedly as people age, their frontal lobes weaken. This is why the stereotype of the senior citizen who blurts out whatever is on his mind exists. Postsurgery, my frontal-lobe-impaired emotions fluctuated wildly. They ran the scale from deep gratitude for my life to sadness over not being able to function fully. I dreaded that everything had changed and I had no control over any of it.

My mood swings began to take a toll on our empathetic dog. In spite of all he went through before we found him, he'd gradually acquired more trust in me and confidence in my strength. His resiliency, complex intelligence, and engaging personality had enabled him to form a whole and healthy emotional life. But for every step I took forward in my recovery, Leaf seemed to be taking two steps back. He was regressing into the anxious dog who could rely on no one but himself for protection.

Probably feeling like I was no longer on the job as Alpha of our household, he stepped up his alertness. Prior to my surgery, with the help of treats and rewards whenever anyone came to the house, he'd started to display less fearfulness and was acting friendlier to strangers when we walked around the neighborhood or played at the dog park. After my

surgery he reverted to growling at visitors and barking until they left or flinching at anyone who unexpectedly tried to pet him.

It seemed like he was campaigning for Alpha Dog of the World again. If Linda took him out for exercise, his eyes darted around warily as if expecting to fight attackers behind every tree. His regression made it clear that healing from his own past traumas and now dealing with mine was depleting his emotional reserves.

"What's happening, pup?" I asked him one day. He sat on the couch next to me and looked out the front window. He had just gone ballistic at a delivery truck that drove by our house. He hurled his body so hard against the picture window that I thought he might have broken a rib. I had to run my hands along his ribcage to make sure everything was still intact.

This was a dog who needed to feel secure and safe. He had to know he could rely on me. But I was in no condition for anyone to rely on me for anything.

As my days recovering at home dwindled, I was grateful to my publisher, editor, and literary agent for not panicking when I told them about the brain surgery. Our editor had sent us a card and gift certificate for a visit to our favorite restaurant. Since I'd soon be thrust back into the business world and also wanted to give Linda a break from caring for me, I suggested that we use the gift certificate before I returned to work.

We drove to a cheery restaurant in downtown Minneapolis. Its menu of organic foods, white tablecloths, and wide glass walls that allowed for people-watching made eating there a special occasion. After ordering our meals I looked at our predominantly green-filled plate and said, "It feels like we're on Sesame Street. This meal is being brought to you by the color green."

Linda laughed. It felt good to have a lighthearted conversation that didn't revolve around medications, looming medical bills, my job, the next

deadline for a book, or Leaf and his issues. We raised our glasses of Perrier and clinked them together. My heart filled with gratitude. Maybe things would get back to normal. Maybe sooner than later.

During my healing process Leaf became my channel for viewing and living in the strange postsurgery world where my body could no longer be trusted to do what was necessary. After I was cleared to drive again, I took Leaf to the dog park so both of us could relax. With my frontal lobe still not in total functioning mode, other drivers agitated me. I now understood how a person could be overtaken by road rage. To my embarrassment, I found myself yelling at drivers who lingered at stoplights. It irritated me that they crossed lanes too close in front of my car, chattered on their cell phones, or indulged in other poor driving habits. Ordinarily I wouldn't have been fazed much and just made sure I got out of their way.

In our car CD player, we keep a recording of around five thousand people chanting the mantra "HU." For me, it is an incredibly soothing sound. The voices of all these chanters fluctuate and harmonize into a magnificent, unrehearsed symphony of high vibrational sound. When I'm driving I often push the button on the car stereo system and listen to the uplifting song waft through the speakers. With Leaf in the car, I doubly enjoy the chant, sensing that it also soothes and comforts him.

On this day Leaf watched me from the front seat as my anger erupted at other drivers. I was like someone with Tourette's syndrome, unable to censor my negative mind talk. After watching me scream at a bus that stopped frequently in front of my car, Leaf reached his paw over to the CD player. Out of six buttons on the stereo, he firmly pressed the one that allowed the CD to play.

The timing, position of his paw, his selection of buttons, and the CD that happened to be in the stereo could have all been coincidental. I didn't care. I needed it. Consciously or not, I knew Leaf was being God's messenger for me. His act of compassion had its desired effect. I calmed down and let the chant heal my troubled, aching heart and mind. Gratitude welled up in me. My dog had figured out how to supply exactly what I needed to dissolve a passion of the mind I couldn't control.

I looked over at him. As if nothing had happened, as if he did this sort of thing every day, his attention returned to the traffic. His curious eyes darted back and forth as he watched cars whiz by. Who was this dog? If I couldn't register an oncoming vehicle, would he lean over and steer the car out of the way for me too?

Later that day I sat on the living room couch with Leaf in his usual spot. His body draped across my torso, and his head rested on my crossed leg. Although I'd grown over the months to appreciate him at deeper levels, at this moment I experienced an epiphany about our relationship.

I looked at my little adopted dog and realized that we were both emotionally damaged goods. My lack of trust in people, fear of being dependent like my stroke-ridden father, discomfort when people expressed their emotions, and an overwhelming need for privacy all sprung from a childhood in which I never had enough strength to feel safe. Eight years of police work had confronted me with some of the worst humanity had to offer. With its random violence, it had reinforced my low opinion of anyone's, including my own, trustworthiness.

Leaf's fear, mistrust, and mercurial emotions arose from losing everything he'd ever known and being left without any safety net but his own street smarts. Although he'd been the abandoned shelter dog we rescued, without a doubt he had more than returned the favor. I knew now that life had turned our relationship to its flip side. Leaf was rescuing and trying to heal me. This little black cocker spaniel, abandoned and thrown out like someone's trash, named after a motorcycle he detested, had become nothing less than a spiritual giant in my life.

CHAPTER TWENTY-TWO

The Name Game

STANDING AT MY OFFICE DOOR, THE PRESIDENT OF MY COMPANY SAID to me, "We're having a company-wide meeting in ten minutes in the conference area. As a test of your mental capacity, you'll need to remember everybody by name." Knowing his sense of humor—at times, humor only he appreciated—I looked up at him with a grin. Then I checked the position of my trusty tan cap. It covered disconcerting visual reminders of my brain surgery.

I was back at work on the fourth Monday after my surgery, not yet fully recovered but feeling unreasonably optimistic. As far as anyone at the office knew, I was ready to operate at full throttle, ready to jump back into the game. The swelling on the right side of my face was now only slightly noticeable. The dark circles around my eyes had faded.

"No problem," I said, but of course, this was a huge problem. I could never remember names even before brain surgery.

Much to Linda's frustration, I'd remember very personal things about people—some of them embarrassing—rather than their names. "Dropped out of school when she was fifteen. Hates vanilla ice cream. Talks out loud to her cat," I'd say about someone. Then I'd wait for Linda to piece together the puzzle and come up with the person's name. It was an "endearing" habit of mine that drove her crazy.

While I really liked my coworkers, I had no idea what most of their names were. I always felt that requiring nametags would be a good company policy for those of us, mostly me, who were name-retention impaired. Instead, I had to know their names strictly by memory. This didn't happen in the best of times. And these were not the best of times.

"You do know I couldn't remember their names *before* surgery," I reminded the president. "And you always have new people around here."

He smiled and said, "No worries," and walked away.

I glanced back at my computer screen and our network's empty log-in fields, then down at my photo of Leaf. It was the same picture that had been on my desk the day I got the news about my unruptured brain aneurysm from the neurologist. I imagined that right about now, Leaf would be curled up on the couch, snoring and dreaming of a chase.

I wondered why, other than due to an inadequate brain, my log-in didn't work. It was a simple password that anybody, even I, could remember. It started with *L* and ended with F, with the letters E and A in the middle. I punched it in. Nothing. Access denied.

I panicked that it was all my fault that I couldn't remember my password. Luckily the IT tech walked by and saw that I was there. He called out casually, "All staff log-in credentials were changed while you were away." Relief flooded my body.

"It's time for the meeting," I heard the president say.

So this was no joke. He really *was* going to make me remember everybody's names. Filled with dread, I walked down the hallway to the makeshift conference area where our president stood surrounded by the rest of the staff.

"Does anyone notice anything different?" he asked the group.

Everyone looked at me.

At that moment any delusion of being at full throttle evaporated. No longer able to rely on my core beliefs, I felt like a ghost of the man I had been. I fumbled with my cap to make sure it still covered my incision.

"We're all very happy that you're back," the president said with enthusiasm.

These fifteen or so men and women I'd worked with for over three years clapped and smiled. They expressed heartfelt happiness that I'd survived and returned. Many came up later and personally told me they were glad I would be OK.

From that point on, each of them did their part to provide a soft landing for me. My boss was able to reduce my stressful workload when colleagues offered to take on some of my clients. I will always appreciate everyone who helped and welcomed me back to Planet Day Job. With more optimism than I'd felt in a long time, I could let myself hope that things would get back to normal in record time.

But progress was slow. During that first week at work, I grew increasingly concerned over my inability to focus. I could no longer count on my memory to kick in. Incessant headaches continued to pound my thought processes into submission. Now, it wasn't only names I couldn't remember. I had a tough time instantly recalling details of clients and job sites as well.

I'd come to the office every day, sit at my desk, and struggle to stand tall on a wobbling brain stem.

Prior to the surgery I was asked and had agreed to lead software implementation and training at a client site in North Carolina. This meant that at only the fifth week after my operation, I'd have to go to the airport, get on a plane, and drive a rental car to the site. To add to the tension, it was a troubled site with unresolved client issues. For reasons I've never understood, I had a reputation for handling thorny problems with diplomacy.

I made reservations for my flight and rental car. But in my heart I knew I wasn't nearly ready for this assignment. Linda pleaded with me to stay home. "It's too soon," she said. "What if you have a relapse? What if you have a stroke? What if there is internal bleeding? Will you be near a hospital that has a neurosurgeon on staff? Will they know what to do with someone who had brain surgery only a month ago?"

Of course, she was right to be concerned. But the site and this big client were a major key to my division remaining open. Now that the merger had occurred, if our division lost money, we'd all be unemployed.

And so only a month after surgery, I sat on a plane, head wound and all, and flew to North Carolina. I had to be able to communicate effectively about the best ways to use our complex software systems. If I failed, I'd be labeled as dead weight at the site. With that kind of client feedback, I was sure that my employer would view me negatively.

Sitting in a window seat, I looked out at the clouds and tried to relax. Clouds weren't doing it for me, so I closed my eyes and thought about Leaf and our favorite sanctuary—the large dog park by the river. Our adventures together exploring the wooded paths, hills, and river beaches brought a smile to my face. I recalled watching my canine problem-solving specialist make decisions about what direction to explore and which dogs to befriend. As usual, I counted on him to mirror back to me solutions and issues I couldn't see in myself. So far, our lives had run uncannily parallel paths. During my recovery I had become even more observant of how Leaf dealt with challenges.

By the time we landed in North Carolina, the steroids I was still taking for healing had worn off. I was bombarded by loud noises from every direction. Adding to my already shaky nerves, the steroids made me feel as if at any moment someone might physically attack me. I again admitted to myself that although it had taken courage to keep my commitment, I truly was not in tip-top shape for traveling or for handling the subtleties of meeting our client's needs.

I thought of Leaf, who was not really in tip-top shape for swimming in a river with strong currents because of his short legs. Like him, I was determined to succeed. I'd do my best to restrain my frontal-lobe outbursts.

After checking in at the hotel, I did what Leaf might have done: I strategized for my own well-being. "When I am not on-site, I will be in bed sleeping," I said out loud to myself. I decided for the entire week,

anytime I wasn't working, I'd sleep. I searched the Internet for the closest emergency medical facility that could handle someone who'd recently
had brain surgery. The University of North Carolina Medical Center was
nearby. I took a dry run and checked out the emergency room. At some
level I knew I wouldn't need to make that trip or require an ambulance to
transport me, but I prepared for it anyway.

Twice during that week I found myself in a state of paranoia. At the
hotel I curled up in a corner of the room and stared at the bolted and
locked door to make sure intruders didn't break in and steal my food. I
was ravenously hungry. Like a feral animal, I gobbled down dinner from
a fast-food restaurant.

After a couple of days, the irrational episodes subsided. To regain
balance, I'd call Linda and she'd hold the receiver to Leaf's ear. I'd tell

him how much I loved and missed him. I tried to contain my emotional breakdowns to the hotel room but my fight-or-flight response occasionally took hold at work. When someone asked me a question I couldn't immediately answer, I didn't know what to do and panicked. In my mind the world had turned treacherous, so the questions could be attempts to trip me up. Since everyone knew me from previous visits to this site, if they noticed my hesitation, they were polite enough not to say anything,

Somehow I managed to call upon every ounce of energy and resourcefulness I had left to solve my client's software issues and alleviate their concerns. By the end of the week, I'd fulfilled my commitment. I was more than ready to go home.

Chapter Twenty-Three

The Retreat

HAGGARD BUT FEELING TRIUMPHANT, I MADE IT BACK TO MINNEAPOLIS from the North Carolina job. Mercifully, I could work from home for a while without the need for more travel.

Linda and I were on a tight deadline to respond to a request from our editors. I insisted that she take some much-needed time away by herself. I wanted her to be able to unwind and sort through all that had happened. After doing some research I found a serene lakeside cottage that was reasonably priced and only a few hours from our home.

On the way to the cottage, we stopped at a nearby restaurant overlooking a pristine lake. From our table on the balcony we had all to ourselves, I watched the ripples where ducks and geese had landed on the calm lake. The occasional sound of a loon singing to his flock punctuated the stillness. I looked at the dark circles under Linda's eyes. They reminded me of the image I'd seen in my mirror that morning. My face had aged considerably since the surgery. I'd acquired a thatch of new gray hair that had grown over the incision site. We both looked as if we had been through a long, hard-fought battle.

"What do you think is next?" I asked.

Linda looked up from her menu. "You're alive. That's a good place to start," she said with a slight smile. "And I'm on a writer's retreat to finish our edits and relax." Her face lit up as she spoke. Taking time away from our incessant lists of things to do was the kind of change we'd promised each other before my operation.

As we ate our meal, we chatted but became silent toward the end, immersed in our own thoughts.

I did feel different. I appreciated the fact that I could make new choices. I knew I had a lot more living to do. I resolved to do it now with a carefree feeling of gratitude and love.

Later that week a truck pulled up and parked near the sidewalk in front of our house. Our yellow cockatiel Sunshine shrieked an alarm. *Someone is trying to invade our home!* His call to arms alerted Leaf to hurl his body against the door. Leaf made his deepest and most ferocious-sounding bark to ward off the intruder.

I opened the door as Leaf banged his nose against my ankles. A young man in jeans and a T-shirt told me he had a delivery for me that my wife had ordered. I put Leaf in his crate just to be safe.

While Sunshine and Leaf continued making a racket, a second man helped the first one carry a comfortable-looking, royal-blue, cloth lounger chair into my room. They took away the old and worn tan vinyl chair I'd used for over a decade.

Right after the deliverymen left, I called the cottage where Linda was staing for her retreat to thank her for the gift. She said that the new chair was to celebrate my promise to rest and take more time for reflection.

Of course, Leaf and I had to test-drive the new model. "Leaf, this is for us!" I told him, feeling like a kid with a new toy. After sitting down and pulling the lever to raise my feet, I invited him to hop aboard. We claimed the chair as our new daily retreat spot.

"It is perfect for us," I told Leaf and gently ran my hands along the soft fur on his back. He closed his eyes and drifted into a doggy nap. His body's warmth made me feel that all was right in my world.

The special soft chair transformed into a favorite place for Leaf and me to regroup. Each morning I relaxed and spent quiet time contemplating with my dog. I wrote in my journal while Leaf pressed his head against my heart and snored. He did not mind that I used his body as a tabletop for journal writing.

The blue chair symbolized a fresh start. I made a point each day of writing whatever I felt grateful for, in general or from the previous day. The practice of contemplation folded me in its arms each morning and carried me to a mountaintop perspective. I began to see what had appeared to be separate pieces of my life connecting into a unified mosaic.

Childhood as part of a military family; finding a spiritual path; my own military service, college days as an underfunded student; my father's stroke and enmity toward me; the highs and lows of police work; meeting Linda and adopting our children; moving to Minnesota, starting Angel Animals Network; adopting Leaf and our other pet family members; an aneurysm and brain surgery—all these moments had been essential for me to arrive at this point in my life's journey.

I was able to identify patterns of loss and distrust threaded throughout each major moment. Now here I sat with an amazing canine companion who shared many of my issues. Our paths had crossed at exactly the right place, the right time, and under the right circumstances for us to help each other heal. I marveled at the simplicity and beauty of a divine plan in which there were no coincidences or accidents, only incredible opportunities for growing into the person I was always meant to be. And for Leaf growing into the dog he was meant to be.

Who knew? I could have never predicted that a rescued cocker spaniel would become a catalyst for my spiritual growth or that he'd open my heart to new possibilities that lay ahead.

❧

Just as I was getting somewhat used to Linda being away and enjoying my downtime with Leaf, I got an unexpected jolt from a hospital surgeon. I had called him to ask if it was time to remove the metal IVC filter that

had been embedded in my vein. The doctor who did the emergency insertion of the filter told me that I should have the filter rotated every three weeks. But with everything else that had gone on since it was inserted, I'd remembered to have it rotated only once. The surgeon I spoke to when I called the hospital said I must come in as soon as possible. "It may already be too late for a safe removal," he cautioned.

If the filter was fixed too solidly, the vein might tear when the doctor tried to take it out. It might have to stay in my chest for the rest of my life. But I knew leaving it in could have consequences. It might actually cause clots to form at the filter's location later in life. I didn't intend to take that risk. The filter had served its purpose by keeping a large clot in the leg from reaching my heart. "I want it out of me," I said.

Linda was at the lake cottage, a four-hour drive away. I had our only car. To have the filter removed right away, I'd have to go through the procedure alone. As I thought about how to handle driving to and from the surgery without my wife's help, I concluded that I didn't want anyone else to assist me. I was working myself back to feeling self-sufficient.

I told the doctor I would go through the filter removal without conscious sedation or pain medication. He cautioned that he would start off with no sedation, but if at any time he needed to give me sedation, he would. And I agreed. What I didn't tell him was that after the procedure I'd drive home from the hospital, through rush-hour traffic, from St. Paul to Minneapolis, to pick up Leaf from doggy day care before it closed for the night.

Obviously I wasn't viewing the situation clearly. Everyone I could think of would, in a minute, have offered to drive me to and from the hospital. But they all had hectic jobs that were difficult to get away from on weekdays. They'd been great through surgery and my weeks of recovery. Why impose on them again?

I called Linda and told her about what was to take place. I didn't mention that I intended to tough it out. Even so, she practically shouted into the phone: "I need to be there!"

"There's no time. It will be too hard on me to bring you back home. The procedure has to be done right away," I replied. "Besides, I'll call Aubrey and Arlene to help me if there are any complications."

It would be an understatement to say that she reluctantly agreed with my decision. She didn't like it at all.

I was determined not to shorten the time she needed for resting, regrouping, and finishing the editing to turn in our book manuscript by the deadline. Our editor had waited patiently and delayed final edits as long as possible due to my surgery. There was no reason to make the book miss its publication date.

The next day, after speaking with the surgeon and scheduling the procedure to remove the filter, I embarked on another early morning drive to the hospital, this time alone. I thought it was a good omen that before we left the house, I had seen Cuddles licking Leaf's cheek with her raspy pink tongue.

An amazing sunrise painted shafts of yellow light against a royal-blue sky, still glittering with a few bright stars. I dropped Leaf off at doggy day care and headed toward the hospital. I guess a person could get used to checking in and out of hospitals if he had to do it as often as I had done in the last couple of months.

Before I knew it, I was on the surgical table. The doctor reminded me that if needed, he would sedate me. I said, "OK." He smiled as he admitted that mine was an unusual request.

I watched with interest a live X-ray image of the filter. When the staff realized that I could see the surgery in progress, they covered my view with a blue sheet. I guess they thought I might get squeamish.

The surgeon told me in a calm voice that the IVC filter was stuck. It had been embedded in the vein too long.

"Do what you need to remove it," I said.

He offered to try again as long as it didn't compromise the vessel tissue.

In the background a radio played classic rock music from one of the Twin Cities' oldies-but-goodies stations. I wondered if the beat of the music assisted the doctor's turn, push, and pull of the device. A split second later he proclaimed that he got the filter.

After he removed it the doctor showed me the device. What are you supposed to say to a man who's so happy to extract a piece of metal from your insides? "It's beautiful," I said, and I meant it. I felt relieved that the medical phase of my journey was now over. At last I'd be free. No more surgeries.

I went into a hospital room and nurses monitored my blood pressure and heartbeat. Without the conscious sedation, there were no rules obliging me to stay a long period of time at the hospital or have someone there to drive me home. I was able to leave after about forty-five minutes with stable vital signs. I walked out to the parking lot, got into my car, and drove away. It was not just a lucky day. For me it was Day One of the rest of my life.

CHAPTER TWENTY-FOUR

Meltdown

EXHAUSTED BUT ALSO RELIEVED TO BE LEAVING THE HOSPITAL, I embarked on the forty-five-minute drive to doggy day care to pick up Leaf. Bumper-to-bumper rush-hour traffic bombarded me with truck fumes, impatient drivers honking horns, and people swerving from lane to lane. The bright sun reflected off car windows. What I had just been through at the hospital suddenly caught up with me, and I began to feel weak and a bit shaky.

I managed to get to the doggy-day-care facility just minutes before it closed. After I snapped his leash on, Leaf wiggled and gave a squeak of excitement. He pulled at me to take him home and feed him dinner.

On the ride home a white van swerved and stopped suddenly in front of my car. I quickly slammed on the brakes. Leaf balanced himself on the backseat. Bright sunlight bounced directly off the rear of the van. My head throbbed. I thought for a moment I might lose consciousness.

Leaf watched me from the backseat as I pounded my fists on the steering wheel. I gave no thought about how terrified Leaf must have felt. I wanted to go home. I wanted to sleep. Desperate to escape from the grating noise, harsh light, and chaos, I needed to find a deep, dark hole in which to bury myself.

Leaf quickly jumped into the front seat. He looked at me with such concern that my anger subsided. With what can only be called the intense calmness a grown-up might use to subdue a child's temper tantrum, he gently and thoroughly licked my cheek.

Despite his own anxiety about people who had mistreated him in the past, he didn't cower in the backseat. Instead, he focused entirely on me. His soothing, rhythmic licks and the cool moisture of his tongue on my face settled my emotions. I felt my irrational fury dissipate.

It was as if in that instant Leaf made a full commitment to being my friend. No matter what. No matter how nuts I might act. No matter how much he wanted to run, hide, or protect himself, he would be there for me.

The white van finally started moving again. I followed it and saw that the driver had merely stopped at a red light. His vehicle had inadvertently reflected the sun's rays into my eyes. I felt embarrassed at my outburst. What was wrong? This was not the real me. I thought of my father's crazy rants after his stroke. Had my frontal lobe been so damaged that I'd never have control over my emotions again?

For the rest of the ride home, my brave, loving dog intermittently licked my cheek.

When we got home, I fed Leaf extra food and treats. He looked worn out from all the physical exercise of his day of play. It must have depleted whatever reserves he had drawn upon to deal with my emotions.

I was ready to zonk out with pain pills. We both went directly to our beds and immediately fell into a deep sleep.

The next day we drove to the cottage so Leaf and I could bring Linda home. While playing the score to the musical *Les Misérables*, tears sprung to my eyes. The songs about loss and unrelenting burdens brought my buried sadness to the surface.

But Leaf, my master strategist, seemed to be figuring out how to pull me out of my self-induced melancholy. Even though we had only been to the cottage together once to drop off Linda, my intelligent little pup remembered the places at which we'd stopped along the way. As we approached these spots again, he wagged his tail and bounced excitedly from window to window.

I took cues from my canine GPS and pulled over at each rest stop. As soon as the leash was snapped onto his collar, he hopped out of the car. With determination, he looked around for potential playmates. He left his mark on appropriate trees with whatever messages dogs give to one another. Watching him do his Leaf thing restored me to the safe haven of his favorite word, *normal.* After the last rest stop, I drove on to the cottage, and Leaf fell asleep in the backseat.

While Linda had been away, Leaf woke up often and was fretful during the nights of her absence. When he saw her again, his stumpy little tail wagged in swirling circles. He greeted her with a torrent of kisses. I did too. I needed my wife. I needed Leaf. And we all needed each other if I was going to make it past the craters on my road to a full recovery.

PART FOUR

Transformation and Healing

"God bless him," breathed I soft and low,
And hugged him close and tight.
One lingering lick upon my ear
And we were happy—quite.

—AUTHOR UNKNOWN

Chapter Twenty-Five

Leaf's Personality Revealed

LINDA AND I WERE NOW MORE DETERMINED THAN EVER TO FIND greater balance in our lives. For me, this included early—and I mean early—morning walks around the lake with Linda and Leaf before I went to work. Whenever I wasn't traveling I kept to this routine.

All my time with Leaf at home and on these daily walks, plus our late-afternoon and Saturday morning trips to dog parks, allowed me to observe his emerging personality in a variety of situations. Many people with pets love their animal companions and treat them well. But their lives are busy. They don't have the time or interest to pay close attention to the animals' personalities, preferences, and points of view.

As my healing process continued, I felt grateful to have Leaf reveal himself to me in ways I'd never experienced with any other dog. In dog years he was a teenage boy who fascinated me with his mix of machismo, intelligence, empathy, playfulness, energy, and curiosity.

More than any pet I'd ever lived with, Leaf showed me that animals consciously use analytical ability and free will to make choices. I'd never observed those facets of dog sentience so clearly until I had the opportunity to closely and consistently spend quality time with Leaf. His capacity for weighing pros and cons and choosing a course of action simply amazed me.

Being human, I interpreted his actions from a human perspective. I wasn't privy to his thought processes and could only guess what he might have said if he'd had the language. I didn't know the reasons he did things that sometimes astounded me. I had no desire to turn him into a person and thoroughly appreciated his *dogness*. Still, he continually surprised me with his humanlike characteristics. He did things that I'd never read or heard were in a dog's repertoire.

I had read an article entitled "What Is the Cognitive Rift Between Humans and Other Animals?" in *Science Daily* about a Harvard University scientist named Marc Hauser who had discovered four key differences between how humans and animals think. Several of Dr. Hauser's conclusions caught my attention. They made me wonder if he had lived with pets or only studied them under research conditions. He contrasted humans to other animals by saying that animals have "laser beam" intelligence. In other words, they use a specific solution for a specific problem but don't apply the solution to new situations or different types of problems.

Well, Hauser hasn't met Leaf.

Take for example the Kong. We would buy a variety of those rubber toys into which you can insert goodies to keep your dog contentedly occupied for hours. After we gave a Kong to Leaf, he'd have to figure out how to open it and retrieve the treat. This can take a blessedly long time and provides peace and quiet at our dinnertime. Each Kong is constructed differently. Some have only a top opening. Some have both a top and bottom opening. Others split in half and screw open. They also vary in shape.

We had seen Leaf apply any number of strategies to opening Kongs. He had relationships with them. He growled at them. *You'd better open up or I'll make you miserable.* Then he switched to sweet talk. He kissed the Kongs in his version of good cop–bad cop. He bounced them down the steps to loosen whatever was inside. He rolled them and made conjoined parts break open. He waited until the food inside started to thaw and then tackled the Kong with renewed vigor. He pushed the Kong around

with his nose, batted it with his paws, licked it with his tongue. Each of these strategies he applied to the different Kongs until he found the right combination for each of them to reveal their secret goodies.

So, Dr. Hauser, although I haven't seen our dog apply his strategies for getting the treats out of variously shaped Kongs to opening a can of tuna, I differ with your conclusions about one of the four distinguishing features of human vs. animal cognition. Our dog, like other dogs I've heard about, applies a variety of strategies to a variety of situations.

In addition to gaining insights about Leaf's personality, emotions, and unique view of the world, walking with him around the lakes and ponds on early summer mornings provided a connection with nature that Linda and I treasured. We watched the sunrises turn rippling waters pinkish blue. These outings became my reminders that life is good. Nature often provided my lessons for the day.

I found Leaf to be complex and at the same time simple. *What does he think about?* I pondered while I watched him. Clearly food, play, and sniffing things, but what's this obsession with ducks? If he wasn't straining on his leash to chase them, he was watching them intently. When they dove under the water, he'd look over his shoulder at us as if to ask, *Where did they go? How can those ducks do it all? They walk, swim, fly, and disappear!*

I know it sounds silly, but Leaf's new interest in ducks inspired us to educate him about them. Linda started finding interesting tidbits about ducks to share with him on our walks. After he watched the ducks digging in the moist ground following a summer rainstorm, she told him, "Ducks eat bugs and worms."

OK, so we're nuts. We told our dog little-known facts to make his and our walks more enjoyable. No harm in it. And I was learning more about ducks than I ever wanted to know.

During our three- to four-mile lake walks, I paid attention to what else attracted Leaf. He seemed interested in particular trees and garbage cans. In her book *Inside of a Dog,* Alexandra Horowitz writes, "Dogs don't act on the world by handling objects or by eyeballing them, as people might, or by pointing and asking others to act on the object, instead they bravely stride right up to a new, unknown object, stretch their magnificent snouts within millimeters of it, and take a nice deep sniff." With deep, noisy sniffs and what appeared to be contemplative thoughts, he studied the odors they emitted, then fulfilled his one-leg-up obligation followed by kicking his back legs. Were these trees and trash cans some kind of dog blog, and was Leaf adding his final or superior comments?

While Leaf had to stop often to read, catalog, and comment, Linda would complain, "I need to get my heart rate up." Leaf never had that problem. With his short legs, he had to take twice as many steps as we did in order to keep up. Sometimes Leaf and I would run several hundred yards ahead of Linda. He'd look back at her with a big grin on his face and then sprint back like a speeding arrow. When he arrived in Linda's outstretched arms, his joy erupted with a wagging tail and lots of doggy licks.

One morning when we were on the last leg of our walk, it started raining. Fortunately, Linda had brought a fold-up umbrella in her jacket pocket. She pulled it out and asked, "Do you want to get under this with me?" Leaf must have thought she was talking to him. *Sure.* He immediately moved under the umbrella. The three of us, with Leaf in the middle, finished our walk and made it to the car without getting drenched.

After one of our walks, I took Leaf to the pet store, where I bought food for the cats, the bird, and Leaf. He loved this place. There were boxes of dog treats at floor level that turned him into a determined shoplifter. He often poked his nose into dog toys to see which ones squeaked. The buckets of chew bones were a favorite pit stop for him.

A ten-year-old boy came up to me as Leaf explored the toys. "Can I pet your dog?" he asked. I said yes. Without my prompting, Leaf ran over to the boy for a quick pat on the head. Then he rushed back to the toys to continue his investigations.

The boy said quietly, "My dog died yesterday."

I refrained from simply saying "I'm sorry" and listened to my inner voice telling me that the boy needed a man to acknowledge his pain. I gently said, "It must hurt a lot."

The little boy replied, "Yes, it does." Stoically he added that his dog had died of cancer and lost any awareness of where he was at the end.

Because nothing normally distracts him from a good toy hunt, I was surprised when Leaf stopped what he was doing. He seemed to be listening as the child spoke with such grief about his dog. Abandoning his search for the perfect squeaky toy, Leaf walked back to the boy. This time he stayed a little longer as the child petted him. I remained quiet while Leaf comforted the grieving child.

The boy looked up at me. The sparkle in his eyes revealed that our healing little cocker spaniel had silently, for a moment, lifted the burden of loss from his heart. The child said thank you and went back to his parents.

Leaf reaffirmed my belief that a loving animal can serve as an instrument of something beyond our day-to-day life, a source of love that some call the "Divine." Someone's heart is broken, and God's love directs a creature with a wagging tail, soft fur, sweet eyes, and a kind heart where he's most needed.

Leaf, like me, was healing and becoming whole. As he grew healthier, so did I. And as his heart grew more loving, open, and sensitive to the needs of people he didn't know, so did mine.

CHAPTER TWENTY-SIX

Graduations

LEAF HAD MANY OPPORTUNITIES TO APPLY HIS PROBLEM-SOLVING strategies upon his return to formal classroom studies. He had been forced to join the ranks of Dog School Dropouts when my medical issues started, but now that these were at least temporarily resolved, we signed him up again for what we referred to as Dog Training 101, the introductory course.

Leaf knew how to sit when asked on occasion and sometimes to stay when it suited him. But he needed to be calmer around visitors to our home, as well as to come when called and follow other commands that are essential for a dog's safety. Some might consider Leaf's ignorance of basic commands as a sign that Linda and I weren't very good pet parents. But we had just been derailed and decided it would be best to start over.

"Look at me," I said during a practice training session on our first day back in class. Linda and I were tickled to watch Leaf immediately comply. He jerked his head up dramatically, widened his eyes, and fixed his gaze upon my face. *I'm looking. Got it? I'm looking. Time for a treat. Where is my treat?*

Leaf's classes became the source of fun, as he taught me more than I was teaching him. One thing I observed was that if education is fun, learning commands and tricks are not so hard to accomplish. It was as if he were saying, *Why take everything so seriously?*

He even learned to associate visitors to our home with getting rewards. This was our dog trainer Heather Anderson's bright idea. Don't know why I didn't think of it. Leaf's fears that our invited guests might harm him or someone he loved diminished as he became more interested in the treats they might have for him.

The class met once a week for six weeks, and we always got assignments to practice with Leaf at home. He responded well to the "clicker training" approach, which associates a distinct sound with the moment the dog does what the person has asked him to do. Leaf caught on quickly that a click meant a treat would soon follow. Unlike Taylor, who had watched other dogs in class and imitated whatever they did, Leaf wasn't interested in learning from his classmates. He only wanted to sniff them and let them know he was Alpha Dog of the World.

On the last day of Training 101, I looked at our cocker spaniel and saw joy in his little body. He marched with enthusiasm toward the door of the large pet-supply store where classes were held in a partitioned area.

Once inside, Leaf's nose kicked into high gear. There were the intoxicatingly glorious smells of peanut-butter treats, liver snacks, and beef chew bones. His ecstatic expression told of an altered state of consciousness. The experience, overwhelming in its scope, seemed to make him come completely alive.

As he began to regain his sense of balance, Leaf started toward the toy aisle. The shelves were at floor level. Dogs had easy access to picking toys they wanted to bring home. On occasion I'd overhear a comment about a dog shoplifting on aisle 3. Leaf had very high standards when it came to selecting a toy. Did he like how it felt in his mouth? Did it bounce? Did he prefer the color? Could he shake it? Did it squeak or make some other noise? The store had a smart marketing ploy. I, for one, never got out of there without buying something for Leaf or our other pets.

But today we didn't have time for browsing. Right now, our only concern was that Leaf knew how to sit, stay, leave it, take it, and wait at the door when we asked him to do tasks. Linda looked down at her boy and said, "This is your graduation day. We're so proud of you."

Before he could graduate, though, he'd have to pass the dog-training test. This made Linda and me a little anxious because Leaf wasn't always consistent with following commands at home or in class. Often when we asked him to sit, for example, we never knew what we'd get. He'd consider the command for a moment or two and then decide to comply or not. We had even less confidence with telling him to stay. When I gave this command, I had to thrust my hand in front of his face, say "stay" in a firm voice, and walk away from him. His job was to root his butt to the floor until I swept a hand along my side in an inviting gesture and gave the verbal command to "come." This, of course, was followed by a treat for not doing what he usually did, which was blithely pad along behind me as I attempted to walk away.

Worst of all was the incomprehensible "leave it" command. To practice this, I had to place a treat in front of his paw. He was not supposed to eat it until I told him, "Take it." Leaf did not see the logic behind this other than to please his beloved humans (not much of an incentive) and get extra kisses and treats (this worked). *Leave it? Why would I do that?* Then there was also the fact that Leaf got mixed messages at home about "leaving" things. He had the habit of licking dishes in the dishwasher whenever Linda or I opened the door. No matter where he was in the house, he'd hear the door unlatch and fly into the kitchen.

Linda sounded like the chorus to a love-gone-wrong song as she sang, "Leave it. Leave it." Meanwhile, Leaf licked the dishes like a dog who had never been fed, much less eaten dinner only a few minutes ago. After he'd licked every morsel he could find, he'd stop, sit, and wait for his treat. She'd say, "Take it," and give him his reward. After all, he'd finally obeyed her command and left the dishes alone. He'd figured out that to get the treat, all he needed to do was lick the dishes first. It's not easy to train a dog who is smarter than you are.

When we entered the training room, we saw that Leaf's classmates, all in high spirits, had already arrived. Their nervous humans sat behind them. After explaining the sequence of events for the evening, Heather announced, "You're also going to have your dog do a trick we taught in class. It can be something like 'roll over' or 'shake hands.' You pick which one."

I suddenly broke into a sweat as I looked down at Leaf. Leaf acted like he didn't have a care in the world. I shouldn't have worried, though, because after a few stumbles, Leaf managed to make it through all the Training 101 commands. For his trick, he shook my hand. Heather was impressed as he sat, stayed, and came without hesitation. I snapped his picture when she handed Linda his graduation certificate.

I told our new graduate that he could pick out any toy before we left the store. After much deliberation he selected the twin brother of his favorite squeaky, foot-long dog and carried it to the cash register in his mouth.

All the positive changes in Leaf's personality were making me think about how to be more like him. His need to be Alpha Dog was transforming itself into leadership. His distrust was softening into cautiousness. His distractedness was turning into focus. He was living life without over-thinking things. Even though he anticipated a situation and responded thoughtfully, he no longer seemed fearful of the future. These were all qualities I wanted to increase in myself. Since Leaf so often served as my mirror, I wondered if I too was growing into the person I'd always wanted to be.

One day when I picked up Leaf at doggy day care, I found him in the playroom with around a dozen other dogs all larger than him. There was an Animal Planet television program on in the background, but none of the dogs were watching it. Instead, most of them were following Leaf around the room.

When Leaf spotted me at the plate-glass window, he ran over enthusiastically. Many of the other dogs ran to the window to get a good look at me. I got the feeling they did not want their ringleader to leave so soon.

Two men, who I presumed were employees, stood nearby and were also watching the dogs playing.

"Is that your dog?" one of them asked me. I answered yes and averted my eyes. I hoped Leaf hadn't been chasing furry little house slippers again until they dropped from exhaustion.

"That dog is something!" said the other.

The first one said, "I've been watching how much fun he's having. He's the smallest dog in the room. But in many ways he's the biggest dog in the room. Before he entered, the other dogs weren't interested in playing or exploring. Your dog came in the room with an agenda."

He added that Leaf seemed to have a method to his madness. One at a time, he'd get behind a dog and push with his nose and feet until the dog started running. Soon other dogs would join in. If they wouldn't budge, Leaf herded them into the fray. "He made a party happen." The man said he was so amused by Leaf's ingenuity that he wanted to see what else this little cocker would do.

The second man chimed in. "After Leaf got most of the dogs to run and play, he wouldn't let them rest. At one point he grabbed a tennis ball and dropped it in front of one dog who had stopped running. He tempted the dog, daring him to grab the ball. It was a challenge. The dog took Leaf's bait and joined back in for the chase."

I nodded and said, "Leaf herds my wife and me too. In the morning, he pushes Linda and then me with his nose and paws to the living room. That's where we're supposed to sit and drink our coffee. Then he goes to the front window and waits for the school bus to pick up the kids on the sidewalk across the street. After the school bus comes and goes, he jumps onto the couch and takes a nap. He makes sure all is as it should be in Leaf World."

"I believe it," the first man said.

At last, Leaf hurtled from the playroom's exit door. Three other dogs tried to slip out to go with him. I placed the leash on Leaf after a hello hug. It still surprised me that he'd allow me to embrace him after all the flinching he did when we first adopted him.

He ran over to the main staff counter next and jumped up with his Elvis-lipped half-smile. Smiling back at him, the receptionist patted his head and gave him a dog biscuit, the kind he loves. "I watch him play too. He gets along with everybody in the day-care playroom," she told me. I beamed like a proud papa.

On the way out I started checking the bags and cans of organic cat and dog food, but Leaf would have none of this and herded me toward the door. We were not adhering to the routine! When we finally made it to the car, he immediately jumped in the backseat and settled in for a nap. As I looked at him in the rearview mirror, I remembered the meltdown I'd had and how he had calmed me. How glad I was to see both of us making progress in healing from our traumas.

⸺⸺

Inspired by Leaf's exuberance at doggy day care, Linda and I felt like trying something we hadn't had the nerve to do, something to renew ourselves and our relationship. When a couple survives a severe medical crisis that involves one or the other doing the necessary caretaking, it's important to restore balance. The next day we visited an Arthur Murray Dance Studio and signed up. Mind you, I'd never danced a day in my life.

When Linda and I had first fantasized about how everything would be different after my surgery, we had talked about taking dance lessons, but I never thought it would happen. Our work once again started spilling into our free time. Somehow things were different now. We were learning to rely on each other more for strength and creativity. We were even reminding each other to take breaks and cherish our life together. Not only as working partners but also as marriage partners.

The Arthur Murray dance lessons were a mix of embarrassing missteps and delightful fun, with a lot of laughter. In a millisecond I'd forget the intricate dance steps, stop during a routine, and freeze on the floor while I tried to remember what to do next. I had to go to practice parties at the studio and socialize with people I didn't know. Holding the female dance instructors and other women who took lessons in my arms was awkward at first. But everyone made me feel OK, even when I fumbled. Thankfully no one refused to dance with me.

My biggest challenge was not steering Linda into the other dancers. I joked that the best part of the experience was that my independent wife had to let me lead. Taking dance lessons was turning out to be better than marriage counseling at getting a longtime couple to perform in harmony.

At home when we practiced before the next week's lessons, we moved the furniture in the living room to give ourselves more space. We'd pop a CD into the player and attempt to remember what we were supposed to do with our feet, arms, posture, frame, and facial expressions. My feet landed everywhere except where they were supposed to be. I was so uncoordinated at times that I almost fell over. But my attempts at smoothness only served to make us laugh even more.

Leaf, never one to pass up an opportunity for playtime, was not content to observe from the sidelines. While we did our version of a cha-cha, samba, or waltz around the living room, Leaf followed. He literally danced with us by jumping up and standing on his hind legs. He bounced around to the music with his paws waving in the air. In every way possible, he encouraged me to take risks, forget about looking foolish, and have a good time.

Seeing Leaf dance with us reminded me how this alert little boy watches everything we do and often tries to imitate what he sees. Sometimes when I hold Linda's hand, he walks up to her and lifts his paw as if he wants to hold her hand too. Often when she sits on the couch to watch television or read, he sits next to her and places his paws in her hands. With his paw in her hand, he watches the activities on the street and sidewalk through the living room picture window. How far he has come.

When it was time for us to graduate from our first round of dance lessons, a woman the studio called a "master teacher" administered the test. As she asked us to do various steps and routines, I said, "I'm nervous." I didn't want the master teacher to think our instructors hadn't taught us well just because we might still be klutzes. The master teacher said, "The tests aren't for me or the instructors. They're for you to show you how far you've come."

When I looked back at all this, it occurred to me that there are times in life when dancing, laughing, and playing with others are spiritual practices too. Truly observing each moment as a spiritually rich, intensely enjoyable opportunity is being true to yourself as a divine spark. There's no need to back off from the way life wants to flow just because you're a small dog or have never danced before. None of that is worth stopping the party.

Chapter Twenty-Seven

My Body Remembers

It was another perfect walk by the lake. The sun was shining and the air was brisk. There were no pressing deadlines, no emotional upheavals, no imminent health scares. Even so, something felt off in Anderson World. For the past week our animals had acted strangely and seemed to need extra petting and attention. Linda complained, "I'm so worn out. I don't know why." I was feeling oddly anxious. Although my moods weren't fluctuating as wildly as they had in the weeks after surgery, I still had my highs and lows.

My unease stemmed from a recent dream. With Leaf trotting along happily between us, I started telling Linda about it. "I dreamed that the area where I'd had brain surgery didn't properly heal."

"What an awful thought," Linda gasped. Leaf, hearing the alarm in her voice, looked up fretfully at me. I patted him on the head and took a deep breath before continuing.

"As soon as I realized fixing myself was hopeless, the nightmare ended."

"Do you think the surgery wasn't fully successful, and you're only now finding out about it?"

Linda had voiced my thoughts. We rounded the lake and headed toward the parking lot. I just wanted to go home, sit in my recliner with Leaf on my lap, and contemplate the meaning of the disturbing dream.

Linda stayed quiet while I opened the car door after our walk. Leaf jumped into the backseat. I could tell she was thinking while she poured cool water in his bowl. After she got into the front seat, she opened another bottle of water and handed it to me for a drink.

"You know, I read an article that said the body remembers trauma," she explained. "There have been studies showing that on the anniversary of something dramatic, the body goes through the emotions again. They called it the anniversary syndrome. It's been a year since your surgery."

I suddenly understood why our entire family was feeling and acting out of sorts. One year ago I had brain surgery. Beneath the surface of my subconscious mind, the memories of it were affecting me on some fundamental level. My body had registered the trauma. Now a year later the physical reality had hit me full force and communicated with my conscious mind in a dream.

During the course of the year following my surgery, I'd often wondered if I'd ever have the same brain functionality as before. My memory and my ability to stay focused had definitely diminished, but for how long? At night I'd lie awake, wondering if the doctor's assurance that he could clip anything had applied to me. Had he been able to do the work so that I would actually be cured? Even a year later I occasionally experienced fight-or-flight episodes during which I panicked or felt anger rise up in me unexpectedly.

On the anniversary of my surgery, I thought it might be a good idea to think positive. What benchmarks had I passed? What concerns had been resolved? Had Linda and I made all the changes we promised each other prior to the surgery? Was life better than ever?

I remained employed by the same company, but from all signs our division was gasping its final breaths. I would have to deal with finding a new job. My daily life was not much different from what it had been. The pressures and bills were still there, maybe even more so with extraordinary new medical expenses to pay.

I recalled the Building of Life dream and the vision in which Leaf brought me my ticket. In spite of some things being the same or, as with my job, worse, something profound had shifted inside of me. I was alive. I could breathe and feel and think. I could hug people and shake their hands. I laughed and felt contentment. Having been pulled back from the brink, I ultimately considered myself to be the luckiest man in the world.

Much more than ever, I cherished all living beings. With the aid of everyone who had helped me through the crisis, some of whom I might never see again, I had come to know that relationships, not work or achieving all my goals, are what's important. The presurgery flashes of regretful and painful memories stopped after surgery. They had given me the opportunity to see the consequences of my past words and actions. As a result, being kind to everyone I met had become an automatic response. I honestly did not want to hurt or do damage with a foul judgment or word to anyone ever again. To exert control over my emotions, I'd become extremely careful. I perfected the art of stopping and thinking before speaking whatever came to mind. I felt appreciation and respect for each soul. Without a doubt I knew that we are all connected with the light that guides us through our life journeys.

My moments with Leaf added a richness and joy beyond anything I'd ever experienced with an animal. I made a point of taking him to dog-park heaven by the river just about every week. We explored trees and creeks. He climbed high onto fallen tree trunks to survey the kingdom. I set no time limit or deadline, made no plan, and allowed myself the freedom to be fully present in the moment.

With my dog and my wife, I loved sitting on a fallen log by the riverbank. I'd feel the warmth in my throat from the coffee we bought from a shop that also gave Leaf a biscuit. I'd take in the peacefulness of a flowing river, the birds swooping overhead, the smell of wet dog, the sound of barks and rustling leaves.

One day I watched a man and his young son walking with their golden retriever close to the river. The father was letting the boy throw a tennis ball into the river for their dog to swim after and retrieve. I wondered if they

knew they were sharing an experience to remember forever, moments in time when they felt the purest love for each other and for life.

Prior to my brain surgery and all its ordeals, I would have missed observing this example of love in action. Preoccupation with a long list of responsibilities I needed to accomplish after our walk would have obstructed this image of father, son, and dog forming a circle of love.

Now that I'd arrived at my one-year anniversary, I realized that gradually happiness had inched into and then blossomed in my life. Each moment I could still take a breath had become a miracle, a gift I no longer took for granted. I felt exquisite gratitude for every person I was privileged to meet. No one came into my life by accident. Each had a purpose for being part of my journey, as I was part of theirs.

I found it much easier to let go of my concerns. Very little merited fretting over. For the first time ever, at the deepest level I knew this to be the truth.

Chapter Twenty-Eight

Leaf Speaks; Others Hear

POSITIVE CHANGES WEREN'T JUST OCCURRING IN MY LIFE. THEY WERE also manifesting themselves for Leaf in the form of a new canine heaven. Keith and Patrycia (Trish) Miller had just opened Pampered Pooch Playground, a state-of-the-art doggy-day-care center and boarding facility in our community. After my first visit there, I believed this would be a place where Leaf could become more socialized. I brought Leaf with me to see the new place and he immediately took a liking to Keith. Each subsequent visit he'd hurl himself into Keith's arms and wiggle with gusto.

"Leaf is ecstatically happy no matter what he does," Keith told me one day after Leaf had been going to the doggy day care for about six months. "He's different from our other dogs," he added. "He brings a smile to everyone because he emotes genuine bliss being here. He is saying when he comes in that this is the most wonderful thing ever!"

As we talked, a door opened and released Leaf into the lobby. He danced and twirled in the lobby until Keith squatted down and petted him, while Leaf squirmed in his arms.

"I've seen this guy grow," Keith said, looking up. "Remember, he was one of the first five dogs to come here. He was kind of wild and scattered back then but so lovable."

Along with Keith, the doggy-day-care staff affirmed what we'd observed about Leaf's ability to strategize and get what he wanted. Their experiences with him also reinforced something we had come to appreciate about our dog: Leaf was adept at communicating whatever he wanted, needed, or felt.

"Leaf is obsessed with water," one employee told me. Keith added, "If the doggy pool has water in it, Leaf is there. If the hose is turned on, he wants to play with the running water. If the water bowl is full, he plunges his paws into the bowl and tips it over."

If there is a thunderstorm, Leaf stands in the doorway and barks at the wind. His long ears flap with each gust of wind and rain. "It's like Leaf dares storms to come closer," a staff member told me.

The staff marvels at what a master Leaf is at avoiding conflict and defusing tense situations among the other dogs. Because of his diplomacy skills, among other attributes, he quickly became a staff favorite. Keith decreed that no matter how busy the facility might be, Leaf would always be welcome, because he "gets along with everyone."

In no time Leaf trained the staff to let him play in either the big-dog or the little-dog section. When he decided he's had enough in one, he paws the gate to tell them that he's ready to change venues. They honor his request and let him move into the play area of his choice.

Most of the dogs didn't pay much attention to the day care's humans, but Leaf was different. "He watches us," a young employee told me. "He pays attention. If I leave the doggy playroom, even for a few minutes, he

lets me know. He points his nose in the air, takes a deep breath, and lets out a substantial passionate howl like he's asking, 'Where did you go?'" I recalled this same employee would sometimes carry Leaf in her arms with no argument from him. He seemed to like her personal attention. "I love that guy," she said to me one day.

❦

Leaf's world was really beginning to expand. Our neighbors played with him whenever they walked to their garage or did yard work. Strangers at the dog-park heaven by the river commented on his engaging manner, energy, and indefatigable desire to retrieve balls.

The security guard at the public library near our house told me that he watched out for Leaf whenever he saw him in our backyard. He looked down at Leaf and said, "I got your back!"

An artist saw one of Leaf's photos on Facebook and painted a portrait of him. She was enthralled with the intelligence in his eyes and how he radiated an understanding far beyond his *dogness*. She entered her portrait of Leaf in contests and won top prizes.

It surprised and gratified us when Leaf started communicating with people outside his home and neighborhood. On November 1, 2008, he declared his candidacy for president of the United States. The campaign of 2008 had grown so contentious that Leaf decided to throw his leash into the ring. For his YouTube video "This Dog for President—Funny Dog Shaking Hands and More," Leaf wore his trademark blue suspenders and shook the hands of voters as he walked around Lake Harriet. His Facebook page garnered many comments including those from people who claimed they would make Leaf their write-in candidate. Craig Wilson, columnist for *USA Today*, became one of Leaf's fans. Leaf's campaign became a rallying point for adopting shelter dogs.

Now that Leaf was becoming something of a celebrity, we decided to take his training to the next level and registered him for intermediate

181

training, or what we called Training 102. He not only passed all the tests but also showed his competitive nature. When Heather, the instructor, pitted one dog against another for the final tests, Leaf outshone them all. He graduated with highest honors. Heather named him MVP, "most valuable player." The fact that Leaf loved winning was a new discovery about our cocker spaniel.

Leaf was always two steps ahead of figuring out our tricks to get him to obey commands until we stumbled upon a new strategy that helped him become a fully cooperative family member. If we needed him to do something that wasn't an obedience command he'd learned at dog school, we had to give him a detailed reason first, and then he would comply. But he always required the full explanation.

For example, I'd tell him, "Leaf, Linda got up early to finish some work we had to send to our editor. She's very tired and wants to take a nap. We need you to be very quiet."

Usually this high-energy boy would run from one part of the house to the other to bark at people passing by the living room window. But if I asked him nicely, there wouldn't be a peep out of him while Linda slept. And then when she woke up, he'd run to get his squeaky toy and squeak it once. It was as if he were saying, *See, I could have been doing this. But I didn't.*

"How was your day?" Linda asked Leaf one evening.

His responses were something that sounded like, *Great! I saw a rabbit out back. Ate apple pieces. Stole the cats' food. And barked at the mailman. A super day!* Linda and I looked at each other, puzzled and pleased. Leaf had started talking.

While one of us patted his head, he chatted away. If I touched his throat, I could feel his vocal cords vibrating. He moved his mouth and emitted sounds. He accompanied these vocalizations with intermittent licks. The intense expression on his face showed that he was seriously attempting to communicate by imitating the way humans spoke.

He mostly confided in Linda. At night she'd ask him, "How was your day?" His answers came in a series of snorts, squeals, grunts, and mumbles. It often seemed as if Leaf was trying to say "I love you," the way he hears humans do. He used the same vocal inflections.

We remembered when Barbara Walters confided to her skeptical cohosts on *The View* that her dog Cha-Cha talked to her. She endured a lot of ridicule after making that remark.

We asked readers of our Angel Animals Story of the Week newsletter what words their pets understood. We compiled a long list of words, commands, and questions that included "Want to go for a hike?," "Do you want a bath?," and "Time for bed." One person said that her dog understands key words she uses for him in English, French, Spanish, and German.

I've heard that dogs have roughly a three-hundred-word vocabulary. So Linda and I decided to start a list of the words Leaf responded to most consistently:

popcorn, carrots, banana: he comes running

doggy day care: inspires a sprint to the car

dog park: he's all fired up and ready to go, with his orange ball

up, up, up: he jumps on the bed for a hug, kisses, and a tummy rub

tummy, tummy, tummy: he rolls over faster than money from a 401K to an IRA

squeaky toy: he roots through his collection for favorite toy of the moment

focus: reminds him that he's not in the backyard to chase rabbits or squirrels

rabbit: he darts from one car window to the next

quit screwing around: see focus above

normal: his favorite word

good dog: his favorite two words

Of course he still remembered (well, sort of) his dog-school training commands:

sit: more like, squat for a second

stay: more like, pause

shake: more like, wave my paw around

down: more like, I'll think about it and decide if I want to

For all his ability to communicate with people, Leaf was an incredibly quiet dog. He padded around the house so silently that most of the time, we had to go look for him. He had a way of pulling in his energy that made him nearly invisible when he didn't want to be noticed. Linda wondered whether he had been a cat in a previous lifetime. On countless occasions I'd call, "Leaf, where are you?" only to turn around and find him standing right behind me.

To my delight, this remarkable little dog started appealing to many people around the world with his website, blogs, videos, and social-networking pages. It seemed as if everyone who met, read about, or saw photos and videos of Leaf had his back.

He would need it. He was about to face the most dangerous phase of his life since having been abandoned at the animal shelter.

CHAPTER TWENTY-NINE

Leaf's Life Is Threatened

As THE MONTHS PASSED INTO YEAR TWO OF MY RECOVERY, THERE would be no more meltdowns, significantly reduced travel, just welcome normalcy. Linda, Leaf, and I made plans and felt optimistic about the future. We forecast long and healthy lives for all of us.

Leaf appeared energetic even with his occasional bouts of diarrhea and digestion problems. I took him to the vet to get checked out. Dr. Porter told me to feed him less fatty food and keep him away from the cat food. He loved its rich ingredients. We changed from pet-store premium brands to an organic dog food. It seemed so easy to keep him healthy.

One time while I was out of town, however, Leaf had severe diarrhea and nausea. When he got up from his regular spot at the living room picture window, Linda found a circle of blood where he had been sitting. She immediately called Dr. Porter. He told her to bring Leaf to his clinic.

Linda said, "I drove like a crazy person. I cried all the way there. Leaf didn't move the whole time. I thought I might have to carry him in, but he managed to walk. I was so scared."

I felt helpless so far away from home. I was ready to get on a plane and fly back. But Linda reassured me that Dr. Porter had examined Leaf. He said with medication and fasting for twenty-four hours, Leaf would be OK. "Maybe he got into something he shouldn't have," Dr. Porter said. "It happens with dogs a lot. But if it continues, we'll have to run tests on him and see if it's something more serious."

"Something more serious." Those were the last words I wanted to hear. There were any number of bad things Leaf might have eaten. He dove into the cat food with abandon if Linda or I forgot to keep it locked away from him. One time he found a dead bird in the backyard. Before Linda could stop him, he grabbed it, looked over at her as she firmly commanded him to "leave it," and swallowed the hapless creature whole in one gulp. Any number of incidents like this could have triggered his illness.

On another occasion, when I was home while Linda visited her mother in Texas, Leaf began to have bloody stools and vomit. He quickly became weak and stopped eating and drinking. I rushed him to Dr. Porter's animal clinic. Memories of losing Taylor only a little over a year ago haunted me. I hurried through traffic while driving the few miles to the clinic. Leaf's body lay flat and lifeless across the backseat. Was he still breathing? I couldn't keep an eye on the road and him. Usually he'd be standing up and looking at the sights while I drove. But not this time. Something was terribly wrong.

I thought of all the things about which I could feel guilty. I should have switched him to the premium organic brand of dog food earlier. Maybe we ran too much that day. He liked to follow me from room to room; he might not be getting enough sleep. Had I overfed him or given him too many treats? Did he get into the cat food again?

Even if it wasn't true, I assumed the fault that my buddy had gotten sick. I had to do everything possible to help him. On the way to the vet's office, I played the CD of people chanting that Leaf liked so much.

Amazingly, even though he'd been without food or water since the night before and was severely dehydrated, Leaf perked up when we arrived at the clinic. Normally he hated visiting the vet. He liked the treats but also remembered getting shots. Being probed and examined all over his body by people he did not know unnerved him.

I helped him get out of the backseat. Either too weak to protest or somehow aware that the vet would help him get better, he walked into the building and examination room with no resistance. Knowing how intuitive he is, I assumed he understood why we were there.

Dr. Porter examined Leaf and took a blood test. He smiled when my sweet little guy wagged his tail and lifted his head to look into the vet's eyes. The vet tech also smiled. But neither could hide their concern. "Leaf is in trouble," the vet said.

He gave Leaf a shot of antibiotics and administered another shot that countered Leaf's rapid dehydration. He also inserted a tube into the back of his neck, under the skin, and infused a large amount of fluid into it. Leaf's back neck area instantly ballooned by over two inches with fluid.

"Don't give Leaf anything to eat for twenty-four hours. After that he's going to have to stay on a prescription diet food until we get the test results. I suspect he has pancreatitis. The test results will be back soon. It often occurs with cocker spaniels."

I left the office with a handful of prescriptions, a bag of special diet food, a dog whose neck had ballooned to the size of a grapefruit, and the heaviest of hearts. After getting Leaf settled I did as I had with my brain aneurysm. I scoured the Internet looking for reliable sources on the life-threatening illness we faced.

I wrote about Leaf's emergency in our weekly newsletter and blog. People from all over the world responded with advice and offers of prayers. Leaf had touched the hearts of strangers who felt as if they knew him. Stories and photos of the special dog who had been through so much in his young life elicited concern as he faced his greatest threat. I was deeply moved by the support of so many people.

But along with the good wishes came the horror stories from people whose dogs had died from pancreatitis. Evidently it can strike fast, and dogs need immediate medical attention to survive it. One poor woman wrote that her dog had vomited and had diarrhea in the morning. Not knowing how serious it was or that her dog had pancreatitis, she decided to see if he got better on his own. She would take him to the vet the next morning. But that night, he died.

When the blood tests returned, they revealed that Leaf did have pancreatitis. Dr. Porter told us that every episode of pancreatitis is dangerous and worthy of concern but mostly not fatal. Fortunately Leaf didn't have necrotizing pancreatitis, which is difficult or impossible to treat successfully. Dr. Porter cautioned me that it was important that he stay away from fatty foods to prevent recurring episodes now that he had already had pancreatitis twice. If the pancreatitis didn't completely resolve, it could become a chronic condition that could lead to diabetes mellitus and require insulin injections. So we had to keep Leaf on a strict, prescribed special diet. His diagnosis reminded me once again of life's fragility and how quickly the most important things in the world can be snatched away in an instant.

The days of Leaf's high-fat, rich treats were over. His Kongs would forever be filled with apples, carrots, and prescription dog food. From now on, we had to be even more vigilant about keeping our boy healthy and capable of living a long and joyful life.

Leaf and I had more to do for fulfilling our purpose together. His illness was a reminder that the time had come to amp up my level of service. I was ready to tell the world about the spiritual connection between my dog and me and how Leaf and I had saved each other's lives.

CHAPTER THIRTY

Knocked Down but Not Out

MY SURGERY AND LEAF'S PANCREATITIS HAD TAUGHT ME THAT WHEN it comes to survival, you just have to keep going. Leaf came to our home filled with fears related to abandonment and being ripped from all that was familiar. At the dog park, at home, in pet stores, and out on neighborhood walks, he was forced to confront things that frightened him. His indomitable spirit enriched my own growth, as I watched and learned from how courageously he handled life's daily challenges.

"Time for our walk," I said with a smile, as Leaf wiggled and gave me his Elvis lip. The park I had chosen for this day had several soccer fields, a baseball field, a children's playground, a paved walking trail, and a small pond for the ducks. After a week of clouds and rain, it felt pleasant to be out in the sunshine and fresh air. Leaf and I loved our time together, just us fellas taking a walk.

A half-dozen young men played soccer at the far end of one of the fields. They were about eighty yards from where Leaf and I strolled on a paved path around the pond. When nobody was near, I let him off-leash to run and chase his ball.

When we ended the exercise portion of our walk, I hooked the leash back on his collar and sat on a park bench. Leaf sat down in front of me. We both watched the squirrels and ducks. After his running he needed a good rest. We stayed for about fifteen minutes and then began to walk back home.

While Leaf was doing his "business," a speeding soccer ball dropped out of the cloudless blue sky. But I was too late to stop it. With a thud, it hit poor Leaf in his midsection and knocked him down, flat on the ground. I crouched down to see if he was OK. No worries. He immediately got up, shook his head, and resumed his business. He looked over his shoulder at me as if to say, *Stuff happens.*

The soccer players ran across the field toward us. "Is he OK?" the ball kicker asked. He petted a tail-wagging Leaf. "I am so sorry," he added. They all looked genuinely concerned. All the young men took turns petting Leaf and asking him if he was OK. He wiggled and soaked up their attention.

After they left, I again carefully examined Leaf to make sure he was not injured. He looked like he was ready to take another hit from a soccer ball. *Bring it on, man!*

Leaf's reaction showed me how victory belongs to those who can shrug off crazily unexpected events in a chaotic universe. It reminded me of an incident from my days as a cop, when I happened to be at a specific place at a specific time.

It was early morning, and the bright sunshine streamed through the front window of my police car. I drove south on a busy four-lane city street, which was referred to by locals as "the Avenue." Old houses mixed with family-owned businesses and occasional strip shopping centers on each side of the Avenue.

I recall feeling good about the direction my life was taking. I was devoting more time to writing, photography, and oil painting and loving it. I looked forward to our family's vacation plans. At that moment I felt as safe as Leaf had before he was pelted by the soccer ball.

Suddenly, I thought I heard a gunshot but wasn't certain. It might have only been a car backfiring. I looked around but didn't see anything strange. Quickly pulling over out of the right lane of traffic, I shifted my patrol car into park.

The blinding sunlight made it hard for me to see. I became disoriented. Why had I forgotten my sunglasses?

The traffic continued to pass by me, as if there was nothing odd about a police officer's car parked alongside a busy city street. *Had I really heard anything at all? Why did I have the urge to stop?*

After a few seconds my eyes finally adjusted to the bright sunlight. I saw an elderly man standing not more than thirty feet from me, on the left side of an old, damaged front porch, near the stairs to the sidewalk. He waved a gun, pointing it in the air. He had a look of confusion on his face.

I radioed in for another unit. I pulled out my holstered gun, pointed it at the old man, and yelled, "Drop it! Drop the gun!" He ignored my command as if he didn't hear it. I thought, *I'm not about to shoot an old man. But he might injure or kill anyone in the area.* I crouched down on the driver's side of the police vehicle and took cover.

He started yelling and waving his gun with more abandon. He still pointed it upward. I hoped I wouldn't run out of options. I asked God for help, for any way to avoid what seemed an inevitable action. I'd had to draw my gun before this. But in all the years of police work, I'd never had to shoot someone. What I needed was an out-and-out divine intervention. I needed a miracle.

The old man's elderly wife slowly walked, with the help of a cane, out of the front door and onto the porch. She yelled something into his ear. I screamed, "Get it from him. Tell him to drop his gun!" I watched with relief as she took the gun out of her husband's hand.

After she had the gun, I ran up and retrieved it. She shouted into her husband's right ear, "The nice police officer is here to help find your money." I radioed in to cancel the backup unit.

As this bizarre event continued to unfold, the man's wife said, "He thinks some local kids stole his money from the change box on our living room table. He called 911. The police never came." In his confused state of mind, the man had found his gun even though his wife thought she had hidden it well. He wanted to make the kids give his money back.

I examined the man's gun. He'd waved it around, but it hadn't been discharged. So where did the noise that sounded like a gunshot come from? The sound had been so loud and distinct that it made me stop the car directly in front of the man's house.

What might have happened had I not heard what sounded like a shot? What if I hadn't stopped at exactly this place, at this time? What would the untold consequences have been with a confused elderly man looking for neighborhood youth? What if his wife hadn't come out to the porch when she did? What if she hadn't been able to get the weapon away from him? I had received my divine intervention.

I wrote my report of the incident and confiscated the firearm. Later, I placed it in the police department's property room for safety. His wife offered me chocolate-chip cookies before I left their home. I was tempted but after thanking her, I declined. "I'm watching my weight," I said.

Stuff happens. Out of nowhere, we're minding our own business, and something knocks us silly. Flat on our backs. And yet we continually hope for miracles, for divine intervention. I believe that we're saved from disaster for something we are meant to do, or to be.

I'd soon have clues about the next twists my life would take. I'd begin on a rocky road but move steadily toward the satisfying path of helping and inspiring my fellow travelers.

Chapter Thirty-One

My Mission,
Should I Choose to Accept It

Since 1996 Linda and I have been speaking about the spiritual connections between people and animals. Articles about us have appeared in newspapers and magazines throughout the world. I have never had any problem talking publically about the spiritual nature of animals and espousing the belief that we can learn important lessons from our furry, flying, scaled, and other fellow creatures.

After each book Linda and I wrote came out, we received letters and comments from people who said that reading it had offered them solace and hope with their own challenges. Many told us that the true stories had caused them to never view animals the same way again. They started taking note of another dimension in their relationships with pets. By allowing for the possibility that there was more than could be seen, felt, heard, touched, or proven scientifically, they had discovered divine treasures in their own homes and backyards.

I told many great stories, my own and those of others. But I hadn't yet shared the miracle that occurred when my cocker spaniel delivered my ticket to the Building of Life. To explain that such a thing had indeed happened to me seemed nothing less than daunting, maybe impossible. In fact, I hadn't even spoken about my brain surgery to anyone outside my immediate circle of family, friends, and coworkers.

When I first went back to work, a coworker visited me in my office. He spoke quietly, looking over his shoulder to make sure no one else was listening. "I've had brain surgery too," he said. "It's not something I talk about. People look at you differently, you know. Like there's got to be something wrong with you because a doctor has operated on your brain." I understood exactly what he was saying. I knew that I'd have to work hard to show them all that the surgery hadn't diminished or changed me in how I did my job.

As far as the spiritual element of my healing journey with Leaf, this was even more difficult to share with others. Everyone has his or her own beliefs. I respect that and have no desire to convert anyone to my way of thinking. For me, it started at an early age. My spiritual experiences and profound dreams, which were as meaningful as anything that occurred while I was awake, helped me understand the richness of my inner life. I recorded them in journals and attempted to understand dreams not only as coming from my subconscious but as spiritual messages for me to contemplate. They prepared me to accept as real what had happened with me and Leaf.

Not so for everyone else. Many people assume that these types of experiences or prophetic dreams only happened to holy men and women of old. Could everyday people today be touched by grace too? My theory was that if you had a spiritual experience, you didn't talk about it for a number of reasons. You wanted to avoid ridicule. You discounted what happened because you couldn't prove or duplicate it. Or you believed that others would think you were crazy. Linda once mentioned to a very pragmatic friend of hers that Leaf had saved my life. The man immediately quipped, "So was the dog in the operating room with Allen?"

As a matter of fact, he was in the operating room. I felt his presence there as clearly and truly as if someone had carried his wiggly body in to lick my cheek before I went under the anesthesia. But how could I talk to others about this without sounding insane? Being an innately private person, I knew it would take courage for me to trust that if I gave a talk about my healings with Leaf, I could be laughed offstage. But wouldn't speaking in public about the assistance of my dog help others who suffered from the blows and tragedies of life?

I finally had to come to terms with the fact that my mission, should I choose to accept it, would be to shine light in dark places. If I were to keep the commitment Linda and I had made to spend the rest of my life bringing more love into the world, I had to tell my own story with conviction and detachment. Whether anyone believed it or not or thought my brain surgery had made me lose touch with reality simply didn't matter. Through my story of Leaf, I had to at least try to convey the depth of love and richness of healing that could occur when a person and an animal bond at a deeper level.

To talk openly about my spiritual experiences with Leaf, I realized that I must get more creative. I decided to work from a side door and not confront audiences head on. People liked to be entertained. They needed to be uplifted in subtle ways with lightness and laughter.

I'd often visualize one of Leaf's funny expressions as I gave a talk. This made me feel more at ease and less dependent on other people's approval and acceptance. I engaged audiences by encouraging people with pet family members to share their own experiences, regardless of how they may label it. But often love and devotion from their pet was the driving message for their story.

Over the coming months Rotary Clubs and other civic groups embraced my messages that loyalty and devotion can create a bond between a person and his or her dog that can go beyond the physical senses. My talks gave validation to those who believed they were learning about many aspects of life, including spirituality, from their pets.

A high point was speaking about my brain aneurysm at the Minneapolis Convention Center. The seminar manager had to leave the area for a few minutes during my talk. When she returned she asked one of the people backstage, "Why are people laughing about Allen's imminent demise?"

I'd learned that if I expected people to go on my journey with me, it was an easier ride if I laced it with humor. My story about "the Memo" was always good for a laugh, especially from the women. This allowed the audience to relax and know I am a real person—as skeptical, vulnerable, and confused as anyone else. The audience, after seeing what a flawed human being I was, could trust me to speak with sincerity. When I got to the nearly tragic parts of the story, they were rooting for Leaf to deliver my ticket to the Building of Life.

About six months later Linda and I gave a presentation about my miraculous experience at a spiritual seminar in Connecticut. Afterward we met a man who told us he'd been part of the original team that developed the IVC filter, which had kept the blood clots from reaching my heart. "I never knew anyone who actually got one of those filters," he said. I gave him a big hug and thanked him.

Linda and I long ago joined together as what we called a "golden team." Now when I spoke to groups, I'd ask if they'd consider how each of them could form their own golden teams. How could they make the lives of others joyful and bring more love into a world that sorely needed it?

I'd watch the thoughtful expressions on many of their faces as they pondered this call to give of themselves, to reap the unfathomable gratification of finding something they loved to do in service to others.

Telling my story has been one way for me to increase love and respect for animals. Talking about Leaf is a wellspring of tremendous joy. My hero, guide, and dear friend shows everyone that animals are sparks of the Divine and messengers of love.

Chapter Thirty-Two

How Far Have You Come?

While I had been writing short stories about Leaf for our books and newsletters, I hadn't written the entire story of our journey together during the significant period in my life when I had my health crisis and recovery. In preparation for writing a book about a dog named Leaf and how we helped each other heal, I tried to observe my canine companion as closely as possible. Invariably there were some things I missed. I learned this when I started collecting impressions and memories from dear friends who had been there for us through our ordeals.

Leaf's groomer Patty had been an especially important witness to his positive changes over time. When he first went to Patty, he'd been scattered and confused. But Patty had assured us that Leaf now was friendly and easy to groom. How did this happen?

One day I asked Patty what her secrets were to taking a dog with Leaf's issues and transforming him into a calm client. "I've been doing this work for over thirty years. You have to like dogs to do grooming. It is not something you get rich from. Leaf was a biter," she told me matter-of-factly.

Struggling to get my bearings, I asked, "Did this happen on his first visit?"

"The first year was hell!" she said.

I couldn't believe what I was hearing. I felt like someone whose spouse tells him, after years of wedded bliss, that she has a criminal past.

Was Patty actually talking about *my* Leaf? Did she have him mixed up with some other cocker spaniel? Sure, he had growled at strangers who tried to approach him, but he'd never bitten anyone. I'd attributed these early incidents to his insecurity of being left with people he didn't know.

Patty went on. "If we saw that he was scheduled to come in the next day, our hearts sank. He was so afraid that he peed on everything. He peed all over himself, in his crate, on the table."

Images of my dog trembling and urinating in pure terror made me sick to my stomach, but Patty had more she wanted to tell me. "Washing his front legs was a traumatic thing for Leaf. He did not want to be touched. I muzzled him for some things. His fear outweighed everything else. I didn't want to keep a muzzle on him because I wanted him to get used to things, to gain trust. I wanted him to be nice, but in that first year, his fear always won out."

How often had I been in a similar frame of mind as my distrustful dog during that same year when Leaf had been acting out? Again, my dog had been mirroring me, even though Patty hadn't known about my brain aneurysm.

"Leaf was cage-shy," Patty continued. "If I put him into a crate without leaving his leash on, I'd have to catch hold of his collar. I didn't want to risk sticking my hand in the cage to make him come out."

"Why didn't you say anything to us about all of this?" I asked.

"What would you have done?"

"I don't know, but we're responsible for him. You put yourself at risk. I feel very bad about that."

"Leaf has so much personality compared to a lot of dogs we see here. The real Leaf has come to a better emotional place after a nightmarish first year." Patty's somber expression softened into a smile. "You're nice people, and I knew you were trying to help the real Leaf come out with a loving, forever home. So I decided to continue grooming him, even though I didn't want to let him come back after the first visit. What if

I told you about the biting, and you had taken him back to the shelter?" she asked.

"No. I would not do that. I'd figure out a way to help him."

However, I understood Patty's silence. She cared about Leaf and hadn't wanted him to lose his home. Aggression typically resulted in a death sentence for many dogs. Most people would return the dog to the shelter, where he'd be euthanized. If animal control was called on a dog, the outcome would be the same. End of story. End of Leaf.

"I wanted to help him be the Leaf I felt was inside him. I could see the good side of his nature trying to come out," Patty explained.

What patience and compassion she had shown for our dog! My heart flooded with gratitude. Without ever expecting anything in return, Patty had been one of Leaf's most valuable protectors and friends.

"After Leaf's third visit, I didn't know how I could keep letting him come here. I was driving home and saw your wife walking Leaf in the neighborhood. He was so happy, wagging his tail. Then I saw Linda bend down to pet him. She talked to him, and he had such a gentle look on his face. For the first time, I could see a nice dog was hiding somewhere inside the fear-filled one. Seeing him that way helped me believe I was making the right decision. He had a home with people who loved him. Love would turn him around. I just knew it."

All this time, I had been congratulating myself that Linda and I were sticking with our commitment to Leaf. Because we had refused to give up on him, he had been there for me through brain surgery and my recovery. His heart had opened so fully with love for me that God was able to work through him to deliver my ticket to the Building of Life.

"It took twice the time to groom Leaf, because I had to take things one small step at a time and do them very slowly. I would tell him, 'I am going to cut the fur on your front leg now.'" After explaining to Leaf what she intended to do, Patty would slowly move her hand to his front leg and begin grooming, as he watched. "Getting his permission helped," she said.

This was exactly what Linda and I had discovered when we tried to get Leaf to do something new. Explaining what we wanted went a long way toward securing his cooperation.

I remembered that Patty had told us to talk to Leaf and tell him what was going to be happening at the groomer's. So Linda sat on the floor next to him and held up each of his paws, saying, "This is what Patty will do. She'll pick up your legs and cut your hair. She's not going to hurt you. Patty is your friend." After the first time Linda prepared him in this way, Patty told me that Leaf was much better and even let her cut his nails.

"I wanted Leaf to relate to me as someone he could trust," Patty said. "I knew it would take a lot of time. He began turning the corner about a year after his first grooming. If I touched a part of his body he did not want touched, he started giving me a warning growl. This was a major breakthrough. In the past he'd flail back at me. I could see that the warning growl was a small step but a big improvement. Back then, Leaf was a dog too afraid to show his nice side, but I knew he had one."

"How could you tell?" I asked, with visions of Leaf's eyes filled with fear.

"He showed me that he was conflicted. Aggression was his automatic response to being touched. A moment later he'd try to kiss me. It took a long time to build his trust. But he started getting rid of the fearful devil inside that made him naughty. I could tell that he wanted to be good."

As Patty talked, I wondered how to reconcile the Leaf who intensely poured his love into licking my cheeks with this dog I was hearing about today.

"All dogs are not perfect," Patty said with a sigh. "They're just not. No different than people. I knew that Leaf had to work through the emotional damage himself. He needed to relate to me. I saw you and Linda were people who gave him a chance. I wanted to give him a chance too. Leaf is an example of what love, patience, and a good family life can do. Turning the leaves is what it was for him," she added.

Patty seemed able to sweep away Leaf's past with the broad-stroked brush of her unconditional love. I have rarely seen anyone display such love for another being as Patty showed for Leaf, even during his worst times.

"For years now, he has been a friendly, well-balanced dog. He pays attention to other dogs, goes into an open crate, sits straight up, and watches all the activities until it is his turn for grooming. He walks around here without disturbing anybody," Patty reassured me. "He is so intelligent and sweet."

Now that was the Leaf I knew—intelligent and sweet.

"If you had gotten him as a puppy, the real Leaf would have always been there," Patty said. "But he had the traumas of his previous experiences, without love or care, before being dumped at the shelter. This was the way it had to play out, so he would become Leaf Anderson."

At home later that day, I bent down and gently touched Leaf's nose with my forefinger. In my heart I knew he had moved on from his past. After all each of us had gone through, I realized the time had come for me to also move forward. Leaf was teaching me to brush off the dust of past failures and lapses in judgment, get back up, and be present. I knew I would always love Leaf no matter what baggage he carried. As he would me.

There was one time we had accidentally missed an appointment with Patty and brought Leaf to another groomer instead. I now knew why this had turned out to be a disaster for the groomer and our dog.

The next time Linda brought him in to Patty, Leaf didn't want to get out of the car, but eventually she was able to coax him inside. Leaf sat on the floor and trembled.

Patty leaned over the counter. She looked directly into Leaf's eyes and asked firmly, "Leaf, do you know where you are? Do you know where you are?"

Her voice and question brought him back into the present. He shook his head and looked around the room and then at her. He remembered that now, in this moment, he was safe.

It had been a profound moment for Linda. She told me later, "Patty reminded Leaf to be present. No matter what happened in the past, in the present everything is OK. I hope I always remember her question, 'Do you know where you are?' It will remind me to stay present when I'm anticipating the future. Or letting the past cloud my vision."

After my surgery, when Linda and I took dance lessons, the master teacher had told us, "The test is for you. To find out how far you have come." The test with Leaf was for him—and for me. My dog had come further in recovering from emotional trauma than I'd ever suspected. The power of love is the greatest healer of all.

⁓⁓

A dear and wise friend I consider to be my spiritual teacher once told me that each moment in life is a snapshot in time. He said the moment is often gone before we are ready to see it. I was rushed when he told me this and didn't at first understand the underlying truth behind his words. But I sensed his concept of life had meaning for the book I was writing about Leaf.

During a week of vacation, I wanted to think about how this viewpoint could apply to me, Linda, and Leaf. Inwardly I asked for a deeper understanding and how I might embrace it for the rest of my life.

Linda went to visit our children in Atlanta and then her mother in Texas. Every morning during the week while she was away, I took Leaf to our special place, the dog park next to the Mississippi River. As always, our visits were filled with adventure, while the two of us explored trails and riverside beaches. I noticed that Leaf would look directly at the faces of people passing by as if he were taking their snapshots. He'd lift his head high and focus his undivided attention on each person. Many seemed surprised that they were being acknowledged with eye-to-eye contact by a dog and made comments like "There's a lot going on with that dog," or "What an interesting personality—such a character," and "His eyes are so beautiful!" Almost every person smiled at Leaf and then at me. Their eyes grew brighter. I could tell that their chance encounter with a little cocker spaniel had made them feel more alive.

There is a saying that "soul equals soul," meaning that no matter what body we each have or our status in life, at the spiritual level we are all equal. Leaf and the people he passed had experienced that age-old wisdom, whether it registered with them or not. During a snapshot in time, their two souls met as equals. But then the moment slipped away, and the snapshot faded from memory.

I looked at Leaf and recognized him for what he is: a heroic soul from heaven in a small dog's body.

Epilogue

SEVEN-YEAR-OLD LEAF CURLS UP NEXT TO ME ON OUR LIVING ROOM couch with his head propped on my knee. He has matured into a fine gentleman who is devoted and still incapable of hiding his happiness. If I lift up his ears, on their underside I can see threads of white hair mixed within the curly black. He's getting older, and so am I. Each day I have been given to spend with him is a day I cherish. He is a fully well-adjusted member of our family.

Gently, I stroke the fur along his spine and whisper, "Leaf, you are the best." Bleary-eyed, he looks up at me, and I feel his love. We are two souls who entered each other's lives when we most needed the healing power of human-animal friendship.

Leaf loves it when we touch him now. Even strangers can pet Leaf as long as they don't lurch at him and attempt to grasp his cute head in their hands. When someone displays that level of rudeness and attempts to invade his space, we show the person how to approach Leaf, or any dog, so as not to appear threatening.

My hope is that anyone who reads this book will be reminded of dogs they have loved. Perhaps these pages will inspire and nudge them into thoughts about the spiritual significance of the dogs in their lives. Maybe readers will ask themselves, as I have, Why this dog? Why now? and be enlightened by the answers.

Right now Leaf and I are two guys sitting on a couch, close buddies who have experienced the frontlines of life and have made our way together. The push and pull of the journey has stretched us. But in the end we have become stronger, more trusting and loving. We're better at getting back up after life knocks us down. We're ready for whatever the new day brings.

Acknowledgments

I AM DEEPLY GRATEFUL FOR THE LOVE OF MY LIFE, MY WIFE LINDA Anderson. Her amazing talents and experience, plus her unwavering work ethic, have brought more love to this world, especially in our appreciation for animals. She was often our anchor in life as Leaf and I faced our challenges. Linda is nothing less than outstanding in everything she touches.

I also give my sincere thanks and appreciation to my editor at Lyons Press, Holly Rubino, who saw in this book the dual journey of Leaf and me as a story that many would relate to and with her skillful editing made my story flow with precision and grace. I would like to thank the staff at Lyons Press including marketing director Shana Capozza, our efficient and enthusiastic project editor Julie Marsh, cover designer Libby Kingsbury, interior designer Sheryl P. Kober, the book's layout artists Sue Murray and Melissa Evarts, publicist Jessica DeFranco, and executive director of editorial Janice Goldklang.

I extend my heartfelt gratitude to Stephanie Kip Rostan of Levine Greenberg Literary Agency Inc., our energetic, patient, and astute literary agent who believed in this book and found the right publisher for it.

A special thanks to an individual who lives by the code of unconditional love, Patty Anderson of the Dog House grooming. She became Leaf's close friend under circumstances most would walk away from. Thank you, Patty.

Thank you Keith and Patrycia (Trish) Miller for making Leaf and us feel welcome anytime at Pampered Pooch Playground. As you know, if

Leaf has a choice for vacation spots, your place is where he wants to go. He loves it there.

Without the brilliant surgeon Dr. Eric Nussbaum, Nurse Jody Lowary, and the amazing hospital team, I might not be sharing our story. Thank you.

Leaf's veterinarian Bennett Porter, DVM, and his team at Westside Pet Clinic, thank you for saving Leaf's life when things could have turned out badly. Leaf is a healthy, happy boy because of your work.

It would have been so much more difficult to face my challenges without the help and support of my previous coworkers and employers. Thank you.

Thank you, Georgia Hughes and Monique Muhlenkamp, for the encouragement and help you have given us over the years.

Thank you, Heather Anderson, for teaching us how to train Leaf with positive reinforcement and a lot of fun.

We appreciate animal communicators Marcia Pruett Wilson and Mary Stoffel, who gave us insights to Leaf's emotional state during our early months with him as he got used to his new home.

Of course, I love the Minnesota Pet PAC Group that has given Linda and me support with our books and events.

To the American Humane Association, especially Robin Ganzert, PhD, and pet columnist and radio host Steve Dale, our special and warm thanks for all you do to protect animals and children and for selecting us to help spread the American Humane Association's messages of kindness and respect.

Thank you, Darby Davis, editor of *Awareness Magazine,* for all the years of publishing our column "Pet Corner" and for your constant support.

For many years I spent time writing this book with the Thursday Night Writers, reading draft chapters and Leaf stories with so much positive feedback from group members. Without our weekly meetings, I don't know if I would have been able to accomplish all that was needed to tell the story.

I also did a lot of writing at the beautiful Minnesota Landscape Arboretum. What a wonderful resource!

I want to especially thank my mother, Bobbie Anderson, who helped instill a love for animals in me at an early age. To our daughter and son, Susan Anderson and Mun Anderson: You're the best. Much love to my sister, Gale Fipps, and my brother, Richard Anderson, and their families.

I am deeply appreciative for the years of encouragement from my friends Harold Klemp, my spiritual teacher and mentor, and his wife, Joan Klemp, who started me on and inspired me in my journey of giving service by writing books about the animal-human spiritual bond.

Bob Lawton, you were there for me, and I will always remember that special phone call when I needed it most.

With sincere appreciation for Peter and Sheri Skelskey: You've been an inspiration to me.

I have so many friends who helped Linda and me during my medical experiences. Aubrey and Arlene Forbes were always there for both of us. What special friends you are! The amazing Barbara Bucker is a close and dear friend who often shares her uplifting thoughts on living a spiritual life. Thank you for your friendship and support over the years, Daniel Tardent, Josse Ford, Doug and Sharon Kunin, Doug and April Munson, Tony Luppinaci, Frank Percoski, Gary Foster, Lawrence Chase, Sheila Bontreger, Alden Butcher and Anne Archer, Dale and Lyndra Antonson, Carol Frysinger, and Barbara Morningstar.

And thank you, Kristy Walker, for all your support and friendship and for the beautiful photo you took of Leaf and me.

And to Sunshine, Cuddles, Leaf, Taylor, Speedy, Sparkle, Prana, Mugsie, Brandy, and Feisty. You were our first and greatest healers and teachers.

ABOUT THE AUTHORS AND
ANGEL ANIMALS NETWORK

Allen Anderson is an inspirational speaker and coauthor of a series of books about the benefits of having pets as family members. In 1996 he and his wife Linda Anderson cofounded the Angel Animals Network to share stories that convey uplifting messages about relationships between people and animals. In 2007 Allen and Linda's book *Rescued: Saving Animals from Disaster* won the American Society of Journalists Outstanding Book Award. In 2004 Allen and Linda each received State of Minnesota Certificate of Commendation awards in recognition of their contributions as authors. In 2011 they were named Partners and Friends of the American Humane Association in recognition that their mission and efforts are in alignment with the organization's work. In addition to being

an author, Allen is a photographer and a writing instructor at the Loft Literary Center. He and his wife, Linda, live in Minnesota with their cat and bird and, of course, his buddy Leaf.

Linda Anderson is coauthor of the Angel Animals series of books and cofounder of the Angel Animals Network. She is an award-winning playwright and screenwriter. Linda is on the board of PetPAC, a networking group of Minnesota pet businesses and nonprofit organizations. Linda is author of *35 Golden Keys to Who You Are & Why You're Here*. She teaches inspirational writing at the Loft Literary Center in Minneapolis, where she was awarded the Anderson Residency for Outstanding Loft Teachers.

To connect with Allen and Linda Anderson and the Angel Animals Network, visit their website (www.angelanimals.net), profile, and pages on Facebook, Twitter, and Beliefnet (see below). They invite contributors to send stories and letters about experiences with animals to them by e-mail. To receive the free *Angel Animals Story of the Week*, go to the Angel Animals website to subscribe.

Visit Leaf's Facebook page www.facebook.com/ADOGNAMED LEAF and website www.adognamedleaf.com.

Contact Allen Anderson and Linda Anderson at:
Angel Animals Network
P.O.B. 16682
Minneapolis, MN 55416
Websites: www.angelanimals.net, www.allenandlindaanderson.com
E-mail: angelanimals@aol.com
Social networks: www.facebook.com/angelanimalsnetwork, www.facebook.com/allenandlindaanderson, Twitter: @angelanimals, Beliefnet Community (Angel Pets Fan Club)

3 1901 04546 9527